To

LiSa

Born to Learn

Practical Steps for Improving Self-Love and Self-Worth

Enjoy the read

Donella Hoyle. ⑱

Endorsements

"Donella's story is full of moving accounts of overcoming abuse, harassment and coming to terms with loving yourself. Written with a brilliant blend of wit and candor, this book shows a path to personal triumph." Kary Oberbrunner, author of Day Job to Dream Job, Elixir Project and Your Secret Name.

Born to Learn

Practical Steps for Improving Self-Love and Self-Worth

DONELLA HOYLE

AUTHOR ACADEMY elite

Published by Author Academy Elite
P.O box 43, Powell, OH 43035
www.AuthorAcademyElite.com

Paperback: 978-1-64085-320-1

Hardback: 978-1-64085-321-8

Library of Congress Control Number: 2018944017

To Maurice and Joyce Hoyle,
for their years of unconditional love and support,
gone but never forgotten.

Contents

List of Illustrations

Poems

Meditations and Visualisations

Activities

Prologue

As a woman in my late thirties, I have had many experiences that have hurt, hindered, helped and shaped me in one way or another. Even as a teenager in high school, friends would say I should write a book, since my life seemed to be full of interest and drama. But then whose life were they comparing me to? Presumably, their own—maybe they were part of the so-called perfectly average family of two-point-four children, but I was not. I was born without my biological father around to an unmarried mother of nineteen in the late seventies.

With an Asian father and English mother, living with my grandparents, mother, aunts, and a menagerie of pets, life at home was never dull. I was brought up surrounded by love and kindness but soon started to realise that not everyone, outside my home, had the same feelings towards me. My mixed raced background affected how others treated me—who were too young or too ignorant to understand and who judged me on my colour and not how I was as a person.

As a young child, thugs lit a ball of paper and threw it at my face at a bus stop when I was six; a lad on a moped chased me on the field in the local park when I was seven—with me running away screaming; an older boy called me a Paki on my first day at junior school; a group of men who were National Front supporters chased me on foot through the park when I was eleven; I was racially abused on the bus on my way home from college at twenty and terrified as a result—all because I live in a predominantly white area, where non-white people with darker skin were unwelcome, by some. The non-white population in Thanet, Kent comprises over one percent of the total population. *(Neighbourhood Statistics Office for National Statistics 2012-12-22.)* These experiences affected how I felt about myself in a negative way, so much so that I would bleach my skin and avoid going into the sun without being covered up.

Racism was part of my growing up. As an adult I experienced deception, physical and mental abuse, sometimes a combination of both, from men who either tried or managed to take advantage of me. I persevered on my journey, believing that there must be a reason for these experiences, otherwise why would they have happened.

Growing up was harder than it seemed. With little responsibility as a child, adulthood came as an almighty change. It is little wonder so many people struggle, fall victim to despair, addictions, debt and are vulnerable to abusers. As I started to deal with other people's racism, a new set of problems threw me off course. But it was managing to find my way back that led me to a better understanding of life, using my wisdom, spiritual intuition, and experience to guide and help me to deal with these challenges as they unfolded.

This book is about important lessons in my journey from child to adulthood and how I have reclaimed my voice and self-esteem. I have taken many journeys that were not always easy. There were deaths that I was prepared for and those that were not supposed to happen and growing up quickly to deal with these experiences.

These experiences have affected me mentally and physically in so many ways that could have devastated my life. I prevailed through resilience that kept me strong—not allowing my thoughts and actions to lead me down a negative path. I used these experiences to grow and to help others do well and feel good about themselves.

My life goals kept me grounded, although there were times when I strayed, I returned to my chosen path. It took hard work, determination, and a desire to follow this path that kept me going. I rarely got things right the first time. In fact, most of the time I did not and was given second chances and sometimes more.

I now embrace these experiences and use them wisely for I have many more lessons to learn. I know that from bad there can always be a good outcome, from darkness there is always light and these moments of light are the moments I want to share with you in this book.

Preface

I have wanted to write a book for many years. There is something for everyone in here. It tells of my life experiences, which are invaluable to me, my goals in life, and how I have come about realising them. I wish I had this information, a long time ago, and this is why I want to share it with you.

I have included my journey so far with personal accounts of how I have overcome challenges at key points in my life. There are meditations and exercises for self-reflection and much more throughout that you can do as you read or go back to at a later point. My poetry and recipes are for you to enjoy. This is a book to pick you up and not put you down.

I not only have myself to thank for being who I am but everyone around me whether in the physical or spiritual world. People's words of wisdom, deception, whether spoken or written or their actions towards me whether good or bad, have all shaped me into who I am now. So, with no negative feelings in place, I thank everyone and hope some of my positive energy comes your way.

Having been a Beauty and Holistic therapist for the past eighteen years and undertaken my teacher's qualification, I gained my ACE, A1 and my BA (hons) in PCET. Later in life, I went on to include Yoga teacher training and set up a Beauty Training Academy and teach weekly Yoga classes.

"Hindsight, I think, is a useless tool. We, each of us, are at a place in our lives because of innumerable circumstances, and we, each of us, have a responsibility (if we do not like where we are) to move along life's road, to find a better path if this one does not suit, or to walk happily along this one if it is indeed our life's way. Changing even the bad things that have gone before would fundamentally change who we are, and whether or not that would be a good thing, I believe, it is impossible to predict. So I take my past experiences... and try to regret nothing" (R.A. Salvatore, Sea of Swords). (Goodreads.com, 2018)

Acknowledgements

I would like to express my deep gratitude to Mike Silvera for his patient guidance, enthusiastic encouragement, support, time given and constructive recommendations on the manuscript. I would also like to thank Arzina Hoyle for her advice and assistance from a critiques point of view and I am glad she enjoyed the read.

CHAPTER ONE

Find Your Path in Life

Born to Learn. My hands are to heal, my heart is to love and be loved. My eyes are beautiful and see beauty. My soul is precious. It has travelled to Earth with me already pre-installed with my destination—a path I am still to follow. Born from a moment of happiness and pleasure, I must now continue to spread the love given to me as a child, so others too can understand what it is to feel love and kindness from another.

Dreams are signs given to you to help guide your destiny. Sometimes they are fulfilled. Good comes from them, and your heart slows with the comfort of knowing you have followed your true voice. When you fail to follow your dreams because of disillusionment and distractions, you become anxious. Your path becomes rocky and clouded with misjudgement and indecision. You must experience your path through your sight, taste, hearing, touch, and smell. When one sense is not working, your other senses become stronger. So, follow your footsteps. Reposition yourself back on your chosen path; the one that gives you the most fulfilment. Embrace life and all the beauty it has to offer. Be happy. Be free and know that the time to change is when you are ready to embrace it.

I am a spiritual writer among many other things, and I am here to undertake *light work** to be used for good. I am not bound by laws of set religions. I understand and am open to there being life beyond ours. Life that is created through energy. You are all energy beings. Some of you will choose similar paths—a peaceful one where you are good to nature and humanity. Others are happy to venture away from the light to realms of darkness, hatred, and violence. As a light worker, I channel my energy for good reasons. To help others to find themselves amidst the confusion of being lost and refocus on what is important, to find clarity in their minds and to reconnect with their truest self and go on to have a happy and fulfilled life.

No One Is Perfect

The saying goes, "no one is perfect." This is most definitely the case. If you were perfect, you would never need to learn and would not make mistakes. Everyone would love you, and in the end, people would all be very much the same in this perfect ideal. Instead, you are each as individual as the next person. You may have similar likes and interests and even a similar path to follow or one to share, but perfection is not an ideal to be entertained.

You need to grow and develop from your mistakes, other-wise, you may become self-centred and arrogant. You should set goals to work towards to gain a sense of accomplishment. As long as the result focuses on happiness, and fulfilment,

---

*Light worker is someone who helps others through spiritual work/healing using the energies that are all around us, to help others restore balance and bring energy into their being; someone who is able to feel the subtle energies and use them for the purpose of helping others in need.

rather than outdoing, undermining or making others feel inadequate.

You must appreciate the life you have, as one day this time on Earth will be taken away. So, value those who are good to you and welcome them with open arms into your lives. Some people will like you, some will love you, and some will treat you with respect. Others may cause you harm in one form or another. Always remember to stay strong, for it is your heart and soul that gets damaged on the way.

There is good in everyone, for you were not born to cause harm and hurt others deliberately. Some people believe they can only bring about justice through doing wrong, as in moments of seeking revenge. They selfishly achieve what they set out to do, not caring about the damage and harm they cause along the way. They don't think about anyone else when they are wrapped up in this self-centred state. These selfish people are vultures who prey on the weak, the poor, the charitable, and the vulnerable. When they see an opportunity, they spread their dark wings at full span and sweep in for their prey. That's the way that they validate and make themselves feel good.

You all have decisions in life about who you are and who you will become. Make the right decisions where you can, if you make a mistake, try your hardest to learn from it and correct, it if you can.

Why Do You Need to Follow Your Path?

What happens when you don't follow your path or your destiny? It's likely that your life will have sadness and regret. There will always be many questions to ask in life. As children, you learn by being inquisitive through play, touch, and sight. You learn from what you read and observe and what you are told. As adults when you decide to stop learning, you become old, forgetful, and set in your ways.

The Universe gives you what you need. You may not always get what you want. Do not be disappointed because one day you will realise it was not something you needed. What price do you pay for your destiny? A question you may ask when you are prepared to sacrifice everything—when you have no more to give you will find that your destiny is within sight. You should not expect to reach the end until you have learned from the beginning, to serve, to have purpose, to fight for humanity and bring about unity.

Follow Your Path

Step outside your comfort zone,
Trust your instincts,
Follow your heart,
Follow your soul,
Follow your dreams to realise your goal.

—Donella Hoyle, March 2017

Think about what you want to achieve. Are your dreams the same as your destiny? How do you know what your destiny is? The answer to where your destiny lies is obvious—follow your dreams. Don't be afraid to follow your dreams. Anything is possible if you put your mind to it. Once you start believing, you start achieving.

You may feel you have learnt all you need to know in life. You have your dream job. Everything you wanted to achieve you have accomplished. Do you hear yourself saying, I wish I had done this? If I went back, would I have done that? Why can't you do that now? What stops you? Your destination may not be a stone's throw away, but if the yearning still calls, give in, follow your dreams, become one with your soul. Don't settle for less, when you deserve the best.

What is your life's desire? What do you want to achieve?

And how are you going to get it? What are you prepared to give up for your calling? Are you prepared to risk it all? Is there something holding you back? Don't be afraid the Universe supports you. Face your fears. Use that fear to accomplish your dreams. Use it as the driving force to steer yourself forward instead of holding you back. Whether it is the calm before the storm, the problem and the solution, be fearful at the same time as being fearless. As Walt Disney once said, *"All our dreams can come true, if we have the courage to pursue them"*. *(BrainyQuote, 2018)*

Through acknowledgement of fear you start to unravel a new kind of thinking. It pushes you beyond your comfort zone, into a new type of determination, for most will understand, that fear is far worse, than the reality itself. Nelson Mandela captured this when he said *"I learned that courage was not the absence of fear, but the triumph over it. The brave man is not he who does not feel afraid, but he who conquers that fear"*. *(En. wikiquote.org, 2017)*

When you visualise what you want, it starts to manifest itself, even when you don't realise it. Visualisation and materialisation take time and patience to bring what you desire into your lives. Have patience in waiting for it to happen. In this modern world when you want something you expect to be able to buy it and get it quickly. When those things relate to people, hope, love, happiness, wealth or some other non-tangible asset, these cannot be bought with money. Do things the right way, so you can be clear about what you want and why you want it and be prepared to receive it when it comes to you. Through positive visualisation and manifestation of these desires, you should imagine yourself having these already. With a mind-set of gratitude and humility, this releases your positive energy to the Universe, drawing these desires to you.

Do you want to improve your health? Then think about how this can be achieved. Through visualisation and materialisation—what changes do you need to make?

Find a photo of yourself when you saw yourself as a healthy being. Think about what activities, lifestyle, and diet you were following at the time that kept you looking the way you did. Maybe illness or disability prevent you achieving the level of health you once had. What is it that now stops you being the healthiest you can be? Accept that you need to make some changes, which may be small to begin with to achieve your goal. Creating a positive mental picture of how you would like to be, can change how you are. This positive mental attitude can have many amazing benefits. Like anything, it takes time and patience. Remember anything worth having is worth the wait.

Using visualisation (a dreamlike state), imagine yourself as a healthy person again. See yourself happy, full of energy enjoying life like you once were. Keep the thoughts here and draw your attention back to them every day. Write down how you would like to feel and place your notes somewhere where you can see them.

Say aloud what it is that you want. Listen to your voice as you speak and say the words with confidence so that you believe it will materialise. Send it to the Universe as you say the words. Make the words strong and bold and have each sentence relating to yourself start with the word 'I'. You create part of the reality in applying your energy and thoughts to the end goal. Don't worry if things don't always flow according to plan. It will take time to achieve your goals, desires, and intentions. This procedure will prepare you each time to help you achieve what you so deserve.

Trust in Yourself

Learn how to stand tall,
Even when you fall.
Don't be beat,
Re-find your feet.
Lessons will be learnt, and knowledge will come,
Let things flow for what needs to be done.
It doesn't have to be a race,
Things eventually will find their place.
So, don't give up,
Keep things on the go,
That way your dreams,
Your hopes, your desires will grow.

—Donella Hoyle, August 2017

Do You Need What You Want?

They say the best things in life are free. Why do you think that is? Maybe part of this is to do with your lives feeling less complicated when monetary constraints are not in place or your main focus. You feel less stress and more happiness from a feeling of wellbeing when you help others rather than from the possessions you own. When you reminisce over the good times you had as a child, having fun with your friends, hugging, playing, dancing, laughing, singing, smiling, enjoying life and all the freedom it came with you think of them with fondness. Happiness is said to lower the blood pressure and improve the heart.

In the western culture, sometimes carelessness and over-complicated lives are too focused on money and material possessions. These shortcomings distract from some of the simple pleasures and carefree moments you once enjoyed when you entered adulthood. Adulthood does not mean these moments are left alone as memories. When you spend time with friends or family socialising catching up on old times or discussing the present, taking a walk, walking the dog, dancing, sharing a meal, singing to your favourite songs or even watching a good film on TV, you relate beyond the materialistic aspects of life and become more open to seeing, feeling, touching and experiencing things that cost nothing but are priceless. You again feel what it is like to experience happiness, to love or be in love, have compassion and respect for others, enjoy nature, feel the air you breathe, have friendships that bring laughter, joy, and happiness. Only then do you come back to understand that there is more value in your lives in the natural world and in relationships than in material things. You then take the time to smell the roses, witness their beauty, experience the essence of how the roses remind you of the beauty of life and the environment, you live in.

Being Appreciative

When you smell life's flowers do you appreciate the scent you inhale? When you hold someone close, do you understand the need for love? When you value being loved, then you can fully love. Get to know yourself first, be happy with whom you are, think of all that you have accomplished, no matter how big or how small it may seem, you are still incredible. You may not all sing from the same hymn book, but accept that you are unique, accept that you are different, accept that your individuality makes you, you.

> "Love is everywhere if you are prepared to reach out and grab it!"

—Donella Hoyle, January 2017

Do you fully appreciate your five senses? Do you take what you have for granted? When you feel sad, this may be the case.

So, join me now in this next section for your first meditation. This is the first of the thirteen meditation and visualisation exercises included in this book. Some were written exclusively for the book. The rest are selected or adapted from meditations that I have written already and use in the Stretch & Relax, Pilates and Yoga classes that I teach. My relaxations have become a signature part of my classes which my clients look forward to. My mediations are also available on my website, www.transformyourlifewithdonella.com

Meditation One: Senses

Pause for a moment. Try and safely take yourself away from the busyness in your world. Find somewhere safe to sit or lay down; somewhere comfortable where you won't be disturbed for a while.

Now that you have yourself a comfy seat or place to lie listen to the sounds around you, thinking only now about the loudest sound. If you are at home, it could be a background sound such as washing machine, a dishwasher, a lawnmower in the garden or even the TV from another room. Then try to block out this sound as you gently focus your attention to the softest sound in your ears. Maybe this time it's the sound of your breathing, the inhalation and the exhalation of your breath.

Now work through your other senses, one by one. Let's take sight as the next one. With the eyes still closed what do you see? Is it some imagery that the mind has created or is it a light on the inside of your eyelids? If it's the latter look first at the brightest of colours seeing what colour it relates to, then look at the most subtle, palest of colours here and see that colour before you. Let's move onto the next sense by working towards your sense of taste. Do you crave a particular food and that's what draws your attention to this. Maybe it's the taste of your last meal, especially if it was of a more spicy variety such as meals which contain onions, garlic, herbs, and spices. Or maybe a subtler taste in the mouth, even something sweet like the taste of toothpaste or mouthwash, which may still be present.

With two more senses to go, let's move to your nose to think about your sense of smell. What is the strongest scent here? If at home, is it the smell of food cooking? Is it the smell of your perfume or after-shave? What is the faintest odour here? Is it the smell of your moisturiser, the smell of the room or something else?

Lastly, let's look at the fifth sense, the sense of touch. What feelings do you have here? Does your sense of touch work well throughout the body or have some of the nerves leading to these senses died or started to deteriorate? What feelings of touch do you have? Can you feel your body pushing down into the floor if lying down? Do you feel your sit bones pushing softly down against the floor if sitting? What is the softest, most subtle feeling you have here? Is it the feeling of the back of the hands resting on the floor? Are you sitting with the hands resting on the skin, so a feeling of touch here?

With all your senses working in sync, you are better able to understand and appreciate your feelings, to bring about peace and harmony into your lives. Not only this but by becoming more aware of your senses you heighten them so that they work better for you. You start to hear better and more clearly. You begin to gain more pleasure from the things you do, and enjoy the pleasure and experience which this heightened awareness brings. When you are ready, slowly bring yourself back to an awareness of the here and now.

Practice this meditation as often as you can, and you will soon notice the heightened awareness of being in the present moment. This is one of the many meditations I use at the end of my exercise classes.

The Deluded Mind

They say when you are about to die, life flashes before your eyes and all your experiences, good and bad, like a film, are played back for you to watch. Your journeys and events on Earth are recorded in your mind until our spirit leaves you. You don't however, need to die to see this. You need to give thanks for what you have seen already in life, for what you have achieved, for the lessons you learn and for the experiences yet to come. Sometimes the temptation of riches and thoughts of power can delude you, and you lose track of who you are.

You already have so much if you look around. You will see things you don't use, items gathering dust, drawers filled with things you don't want, that you say you will use another day, but then that day never comes. Yet with all these things some of you still want more. The more you have, the more you seem to want.

What do possessions do for you? Do they make you feel happier? The happiness that they do bring is normally short lived. Objects store your energy, both good and bad; including your feelings of being happy and of being sad. When you pick up an object belonging to a loved one, do you have feelings of them holding it? Maybe if it is jewellery, of them wearing it, or even a subtle scent of their favourite perfume or aftershave? These could be memories or energy.

You are energy, animals are energy, objects are energy—everything is energy. Objects hold vibrations and when you match your vibration, with that of the object you are then part of the unity that it holds. When you become one with the object, you pick up on its energy vibration. If the energy is negative, it can remain stagnant in the air or object. When you first own an object, you release energy into the object and this positivity is released into your rooms, your homes, your lives. But as time passes and the desire for this object diminishes, you no longer feel about it as you once did, and it then absorbs your energy again. When you touch it, the energy is lower or negative, which then stagnates unless you change it be positive again. It is better to accept that this object has served its time and purpose, and now is a good time to part with it or recharge its positive energy.

If the object is a crystal or stone, you can recharge it using any one of these two methods described below:

Method one: First choose the crystal or stone that you would like to re-energise and be clear in your intention for this. Say this silently or aloud, state that you are doing this for good intentions or something like that, depending on what resonates with you at the time. Once you've done this, be appreciative and give thanks.

Method two: To clear and re-energise a crystal or stone, especially if negative energies have become trapped inside. Use the moon's energy to re-energise. At the next full moon, leave the crystal outside in the moonlight overnight or longer in a safe place, to bring its energy back to its fullest. Some people charge their crystals by sunlight, however, caution needs to be taken with this method as it can also cause the crystal to fade in colour, thus charging by moon light can be a better option.

The things you want quickly become possessions, which then add to the clutter of your minds. As you accumulate and become more attached to these things, you gradually get less pleasure from them than when you first bought them. So, you try to replicate this again and again, like a drug. Instead of training your thoughts and mind to appreciate what you have and be satisfied, you become obsessed with the desire to possess. You are driven to own more, to have more, and possess more. To get the same fix, time and time again. *"Whenever we drop one attachment, the ego will very quickly find another. The truth is we have numerous attachments engaged at any given time. The ego feeds on attachments and is always on the lookout for some new thing, person or achievement to identify with and attach itself to." Eckhart Tolle (Tolleteachings.com, 2017)*

When you possess something, its importance decreases over time. Eventually, it becomes another thing that you have. But the thought of someone else owning the possession, breaking it, or losing it, only increases the pain and suffering that you felt when you first realised it no longer made you happy.

So how do you correct this way of thinking? How do you move from the attached mind?

First, you re-educate yourself into thinking in a detached mind-set. Start to see things for what they are worth. Objects of this nature may no longer benefit your lives and may create unhealthy emotional problems for you.

Purposely, try and choose the things that you need and remove the things that you don't. Give away, donate or sell these now unwanted things. There will be less to clean, break, store and less stress caused by these material possessions and less mental clutter associated with them.

When you have finished this process of sifting through the things you need and the things you don't, you will feel a lot lighter, as the stagnant negative energies are released. Let this feeling of 'wanting more', become, 'less is the new more'. Enjoy the freedom that your mind and your life have, in this new-found clutter-free way.

Creating Happiness from Sadness

Depression can cause loss of all sense and reason. You might feel like you have come to a dead end when even a T-junction would be something worth looking forward to. When you feel low, it can be as if you are on a downward spiral, and to shift from this can seem like an uphill struggle. But you all have the ability to change your thoughts and feelings. You need to learn how to do this and be able to repeat it when needed.

They say, "What you don't know won't hurt you" but that's not always the case, sometimes what you don't know is far more damaging. Your mind can make assumptions based on a small amount of information and convince you that something is happening when it isn't. If your problem involves someone else, talk to them. See how they react to what you say then use your intuition. If you learn to use your intuition, you will get better at knowing when you can trust your instincts. It's the little voice in your head that pops up if something feels right or wrong.

Listen carefully to what the other person says, does it ring true or does it feel like a lie? Are you happy with what you have heard? Does what they say make sense to you? Does it feel plausible or does it feel like another excuse? Do you even try to convince yourself that they are right? If you are not happy with their response, think about why this is the case. Is it because you know deep down that it's false? If that is the case the answer to your burning question has already been answered, for your intuition won't let you down when you trust in it. Regularly practicing meditation will help with this by being more in tune with your mind, body, and spirit, which I talk more about later in the book.

As a Therapist, Healer, and Yoga instructor, some may think that I don't feel sad, get down or unwell as I regularly practice meditation, exercise and eat healthily. However, as the popular saying goes, "I am only human" There will be times when I feel sad, and times I become ill as something has put me off focus or off balance.

So like others, I need to find ways to make myself well and happy again, to boost my immune system and recharge. I listen to my body telling me to be a little kinder to myself, to value myself and all the things I do for others, unconditionally and unquestionably. I am of little use to anyone when working on a half-full or empty tank as it lowers the energy I radiate. It is far better for me to rest, recharge and refill my tank to give a more effective treatment or Yoga session—where others are more likely to feel inspired, positive and uplifted by the positive energy I emanate. This restoration process brings me back to being grateful to my attendees for being a part of my journey to self-discovery and development—where I can continue to teach, share my time and energy to help others feel good themselves.

When you feel happy, you experience a state of well-being, contentment. A sure way to recapture feelings of happiness is to identify when you were last happy and visualise yourself back in that moment. What was it about that experience that made you happy? How did it make you feel?

Explore your thoughts and feelings from the inside out. Are you feeling miserable, sad, unhappy and possibly unworthy? Do you want to continue to feel like this? Hopefully, the answer is no.

Think about what makes you happy? Let's not think about a person, but an experience, situation, or moment of excitement and happiness. How realistic is it to recreate that feeling again? Is the previous happy experience you had, possible today, this week, this month or this year?

So those of you who are Carers, Therapists, Healers, Teachers, or in need of some happiness, stimulate your mind with positive thoughts and feelings. Nourish your body with healthy, delicious food. Be good to your body and kind to your soul. Focus on something good happening. It may be a holiday where you can relax away from the pressures and strains of your daily lives.

Spend a joyous and indulgent day on yourself doing something that will not only make you feel good but will put a smile on your face and warmth in your heart—something a little more luxurious than your normal pampering. Perhaps a day at a retreat where you can de-stress and be spoiled, where you relax and meditate or simply make the time to read a book. Play your favourite tunes and dance, feeling your feet moving to the beat, move your arms like the waves of the ocean, sing like you have the voice of an angel and quite simply enjoy.

Whatever moment of happiness you choose, deliberately make that your focus to help bring you out of an unhappy state, instead of those thoughts of sadness.

Say this mantra, *I create happiness when I am happy* (Repeat 3 times).

I have included one of my relaxation techniques here that I have previously used at the end of my exercise classes; to help you along the way to feeling positive and relaxed again. You can refer to this whenever you feel you need to.

Meditation Two: Time to Relax

Take a moment now to gently release and relax your body. Become absorbed in the present moment. Unite your body, your breath, your mind and allow yourself to release any mental and emotional worry, stress and anxiety. Declutter the mind of external thoughts and feelings and strengthen your concentration on the here and now. Each time you inhale bring peace, calm and tranquillity into your life. Each time you exhale breathe out worry, tension and emotional strain.

Devote this time to yourself, for you are important. Feel comfortable and secure in this mindful state. For this is the time for strength to combat fear, a time for renewal, for rest, for self-healing where you nurture and nourish your health and wellbeing. Take each moment as it comes, let the day unfold without trying to change it. Let the moment simply be. Be as you are, without trying to change. Value yourself for what you are worth. Be happy in yourself, be happy with yourself, just be you.

—Donella Hoyle, February 2017

Problems and Solutions

Life has a way of ebbing and flowing like the tide. Then from nowhere a tidal wave can appear that will wreak havoc on your life. This is where your fight or flight response comes into play.

You may all have problems that seem so intense that they couldn't possibly be any worse in that moment. If they were, you would think that you could not cope with them. But you choose, whether to tackle the problem head-on, or run away, hoping that it will disappear. You already know that running away will not solve the problem. It covers it up for a while, until it resurfaces once more. You have all experienced fear as a child, and this has stood you in good stead, for you are here now to witness this. As an adult, you will come to understand that the fear of the problem will fade, once you deal with the problem properly.

So, what do you do? Do you give up and let disaster happen or do you find a way to deal with the situation at hand? Even if you think you would give up, you will find a way around it.

Look at how others deal with similar situations. Some people will feel that other people's problems are worse than their own. When you look at the bigger picture, you may see that you are feeling sorry for yourself, instead of trying to find a solution. There are many options open to you. One is to create an even worse situation for yourself. Imagine what life would be like if the situation you were in became ten times worse than it is now. How would this now seem? The right choice is to think about what solutions you can come up with to deal with it. The root of the problem may not be as bad as it first seemed, now that you have identified potential solutions to tackle it.

Find a comfortable place where you can relax to do the visualisation exercise below.

Visualisation Exercise One: Everything Has an Answer

Look at your surroundings and see yourself looking from an outsider's eyes. See how the situation evolves. Look at each aspect of this, one by one and think about the feelings you have inside. Then come back to where you are, your actual moment, rather than your visualisation and look at your situation again. Think of your circumstances now and how different they are from the scenario you imagined? How bad does your situation feel?

When you are wrapped up in the moment, you do not see how the situation is evolving and how from your ordeal it makes you stronger.

You often get so wrapped up in your life when facing problems that you think they are so much worse than they are. Pause and look deeper into the moment with a brighter light and a fighting spirit, to find a solution. Sleep on it and see how the problem feels the next day. Share your problem with someone close, don't bottle it up, two heads are better than one. The whole experience may be tough and painful at times, but with the right choices and the right advice, you will survive it.

You may have suffered or are suffering. You have all felt pain and discomfort before and it's something that you will feel again. You were strong enough to get through it last time, and now you are stronger as a result. So, rise above your problems. They won't last forever, new challenges will face you on your way, and instead of looking for the problem, seek the solution. You may not have the answer to everything, but everything has an answer.

Find Your Inner Strength

Your problems are only the beginning of what you are about to experience. When your world is filled with turmoil, you need to reach out and grab hold of any positive thought that you can. Life isn't about being a witness to what's on the surface, it's so much deeper than that. To become your truest self you need to experience life in all its essence, no matter how dark the place may be, and how painful the situation is. You need to find your inner strength to realise there is more to this.

From my personal experience and understanding of pain, I will not only rise above this, but I will learn; sometimes by following the wrong path to get to the one I am meant to follow. No wise person, guru or spiritual leader became who they are from having the information poured into them, without having to try to learn as they went along. You cannot put an age on when you become wise, but through a greater understanding of who you are and the world you live in, you soon learn right from wrong—what's good and what's bad, what makes you happy and what makes you sad. Becoming wise takes time, knowledge, careful understanding and experience of the world you are in. It requires empathy when relating to problems that people face, to offer compassion and thoughtfulness through your own experiences, and being true to your beliefs.

You always have choices. Having a deeper understanding of the consequences involved in the decisions you make helps you to make the right choices for you and your loved ones. If there is dark, there will also be light and balance will be restored, but don't go making hasty decisions that you may later regret. Instead take hold of your thoughts, the impacts of the decisions you make and be happy with these decisions. *"Don't do anything that you don't want to do. Keep yourself in a place of feeling good. Reach for the thought that feels better-and watch what happens." Abraham-Hicks (Law of Attraction Resource Guide, 2017)*

Have confidence and courage in life. Some people come from lives that have been difficult, where they have suffered, and where things haven't been easy for them. However, the wiser you become, the more you leave the pain and suffering behind. The further forward you advance in your life, the more you will be thankful your life and your surroundings. You will see a way forward without the need for suffering and pain. Everything will start to make sense and fall into place. Make positive choices and judgements in life, focus on this by putting your effort into what you want. Don't focus on the negative influences around you.

For this part you need to have pen and paper ready, possibly even two pens in case disaster strikes and one doesn't work then you feel stressed before you have even started. On a more serious note have some material to write with.

Write down all the things you like about yourself and all the things you want to have, and then send this out to the Universe, by saying it out aloud with integrity, with meaning with love.

Positive You

Be strong,
Be amazing,
And be true.
Be still,
Be calm,
Just be you.

—Donella Hoyle, January 2017

Hearing Your Inner Voice

How many times have you said to yourself, "I wish I had done it this way, I knew I should have chosen that, why didn't I listen to the voice in my head?" Well, you did have a choice. No one took that away from you. You went against the inner voice that was there to guide you. Everyone makes mistakes, so accept this and appreciate this is how you learn. From your experience you gain knowledge and wisdom.

Have you ever thought, "I should have listened to that inner voice this time, but I will next time?" Now hear yourself say, "I will listen to the voice, and what it says, I will make the best decision for me, the one that I know is right, and the one which I know will serve me well. The one where I won't have to look back and wish I'd listened to my inner voice because this time I will know that I have".

Sometimes, especially for those who are not used to listening to their inner voice it can seem like an impossible task to hear as the mind reels off a list of tasks to do. Forever restless in this state, it can bring about anxiety, weaken your mood and make you feel moody and down. So, try to find some clarity.

Grab some paper and a pen and find somewhere to sit quietly where you won't be disturbed. Take yourself away from the media. Turn off your phones, and turn off the TV completely. Even in silent mode, it would still be a distraction in your life right now. Find somewhere to be where no one else will be around.

Let go of this mind chatter, still, the monkeys in your mind that go swinging from vine to vine, jumping back and forward from tree to tree. Slow the mind down. See the monkeys become tired of all this playing around. Instead of trying to process all your thoughts and feelings in one go, imagine you are resting as a monkey does. You have full control of your mind and the monkeys, for they do not control you.

Make a list of all the things going on in your mind, for these are the ones at the forefront of it. You can review this list later and work through the items on the list, marking each one in order of importance to you so that they are each dealt with one at a time. If necessary, you can re-approach them if they have not been addressed fully the first time. Once you start to deal with the problems one by one, the list of issues starts to decrease, and you will find that the chatter inside your mind will start to quieten down.

The next day you need to allow yourself to focus on meditating. The initial stages of this may seem hard to begin, so don't force the meditation. Go with the flow. Begin with a small meditation practice of around 10 minutes or even less. Try this every day. See how long it takes you before you feel ready to increase this to 15 minutes and eventually you may want to continue to increase in this way until you work up to half an hour.

When you initially start to meditate, begin with gentle breathing techniques to help you to relax and enjoy the stillness that it brings.

I have included a couple of meditations here to get you started. One is quite short, and the other takes a bit more time and is obviously better when you have more time or once you become more accustomed to the meditation practice. Read it through in case there are sections that you would like to use now. When you become more familiar with meditation, your mind will be calmer, and you will find you can relax more. You may well feel a sense of peace wash over you. Guidance will come in the form of a gentle voice inside your head when you need it. Try listening to this voice in the right state, and you will know when that voice will be guiding you.

Meditation Three: Mindfulness 1 (short)

Be mindful of the moment you are in. You may often be distracted by your daily life, with your attention shared among many things instead of being present in the moment you are in. Distractions sometimes happen when you are driving along, and your mind goes into auto-pilot, a state called 'mindlessness.' In this busy modern world, you live in, you fill your lives with so much clutter and tasks to do, that you completely forget about just being. So become aware of life in each moment, your thoughts, your feelings, focusing your attention on the present moment, and not be consumed by the past or the future.

Be mindful in a non-judgemental state. Be aware of your thoughts without trying to control them.

Every time you become aware of the present moment, the here and now, you are again in a mindful state.

Relax without expectations, disengage your mind from beliefs that there is anything wrong in showing your emotions. Go back to the root of the emotion and give this the space it needs to voice, to be heard, to 'simply be', then release it, release it forever more.

Meditation Four: Create Inner Peace

Modern life can be overstimulated with electrical devices, mobile phones, media, technology and a whole lot more. This overstimulation can quickly become problematic, leading to depression, stress and anxiety. You need to reconnect yourself with your true being. Take a moment now to focus on your breathing, feel the way in which your stomach expands on the inhalation and falls on the exhalation. Carry on breathing in this way, observing the rising and falling of the stomach, the chest, the lungs. Feel a sense of peace and calm, wash over you like a big wave of water from the ocean as the tide rises and falls.

Feel this overwhelming release in your muscles that may cause fatigue, and now welcome and enjoy a more restful and relaxed night's sleep. Feel all the tightness, and the tension in your body melt away as you unwind through the nervous system. Focus on your health and well-being improving to a state of enjoyment, where your feelings of being stressed, exhausted or unwell are a thing of the past leaving you feeling happy, alive and restored.

When Things Don't Go the Way You Hoped

Sometimes life can seem unfair and nothing appears to go the way you want. You end up feeling sorry for yourself and think, "Why me? Why does whatever I try to do, go wrong?" You start to feel like a failure, unhappy, stuck in a situation that you cannot get yourself out of. You start to think about the situation more and more until it starts to eat away at you, with no real solution in sight. So where do you go from here?

Well first think about the situation at hand, how many different ways have you tried? At first, you probably think you had tried every way possible, but like your destiny, you have many paths that you can follow, with each one having a different outcome. Obviously, you have tried one way and gone down a route which doesn't make you happy. Maybe you have even tried two ways, and things still have not worked out the way you had hoped. Is this where you stop, is this where you give up? Who said there were no other options? You have many choices in life. You need to embrace them. Try another way and even another. Eventually, the law of positive and negative must balance itself out, so be honest, and pay attention to your intuition. How many ways have you tried?

Instead of seeing yourself in your big boots stuck in the

mud, see yourself stepping out of the mud onto dry land. Land that no longer keeps you confined to one spot but releases you, and sees you looking ahead to all the possible options you have. Leave no stone unturned until you find the best solution for you. Don't feel like a failure. Be an achiever, someone who has 'given it a go' and not let anything hold them back. If it still does not work out the way you had hoped, think about it honestly. How important is it to you that it goes a particular way? Sometimes the bigger picture is staring back at you. It is possible that this is the way it's meant to be, maybe for the moment, for another event or situation to take place. When you're in the moment, and the situation you are facing seems to result in the same outcome, take a step back and reflect on this. Maybe not now, but sometime in the future, it will make sense to you, why it turned out the way it did. You all have lessons to learn, and you must sometimes repeat them until they are fully grasped. So, think about this situation, what it is you have learnt from it? Remember you are the one in control, you are the one who has free will, and you are the one who makes the choices.

Staying Positive

One of my biggest lessons is that no matter what problems I face, no matter what struggles I go through there is always a way forward. So, stay positive, and always show gratitude for what you already have, and eventually, the rest will take care of itself.

When you are in a state of abundance, give where you can. When you need help ask for it, in this way you allow yourself to receive. There's a story passed down through the Gospels called the Widows offering, where Jesus is sitting with his disciples near the treasury, and people donate some of their money. Many wealthy travellers donated large sums of money. One very poor woman passed, and as she did so she donated two mite coins, which amounted to a single penny. However, Jesus commented on this calling his disciples to him, Jesus said, *"Truly I tell you, this poor widow has put more into the treasury than all the others.* [44] *They all gave out of their wealth; but she, out of her poverty, put in everything—all she had to live on."* - *Mark 12:41-44 - New International Version (Bible Gateway, 2017)*

Through giving you help in keeping your energy levels balanced. Giving shows compassion, empathy and an understanding of those who are less privileged than we are. It creates a ripple effect that gets others helping too. You never know there may come a time when you too need help. The amazing thing about this giving effect is that it never stops—for in giving you are always receiving.

With the above in mind never forget that the Universe and angels support you, who have unconditional love for you. The Universe gives you all that you need, so be clear about what you ask for so that the energy you send out to the Universe can be heard and understood. If you ask for something that may cause harm to yourself or others, your thoughts will go unheard for it is on an energy level so low that the angels will not hear it. If they were to, they would never do something to cause deliberate harm to you or others.

The expansion of your mind and soul is a necessary part of the journey to achieve your destiny, whether you remain as a simple being or become one that has reached enlightenment. Let go of your old habits and thoughts. Bring clear visions of what you truely want to achieve and use your mind in setting goals to help you to accomplish this.

CHAPTER TWO

Life is Like the Transition from A Caterpillar to A Butterfly

When I first got married, I told my family that we didn't believe in divorce, under three years later I was a divorcee at twenty-one. When you are young you may have views that make you think in a certain way and believe nothing will change this, then something happens, and it does. It was a relationship where we spent so much time together that we grew apart. A relationship in which I wanted to grow and develop, whilst my husband, five years my senior, was content with his world as it was.

"We don't stop laughing because we grow old; we grow old because we stop laughing."
—*Michael Pritchard (QuotesDaddy.com, 2017).*

As I got older, I appreciated what made me happy, without having always to please others. You need to respect other people and consider their feelings, but not at a price that it damages your soul along the way.

A relationship should be built on love and dreams, loyalty and companionship, trust and understanding for each other. Where one partner feels they have reached a point in their life where they want to be, they should continue to support their partner to achieve their goals and dreams, not hold them back, metaphorically speaking.

When you are young, you have so much to learn. From the moment you open your eyes to see, hearing the world and smelling the scents, you learn to crawl, laugh, walk, write and sing. You simply never stop learning. Like every other human being, I wasn't born to survive; I was born to learn.

My personal experiences have taught me that knowledge comes with age and experience. It is not something that is taught—it is learnt. I have a destined path to follow, as you all do, and I will not allow anyone to hold me back from this. This pathway may be rocky at times and may take you in many different directions, but you need to stand tall as you follow this path and carry with you those that want to be part of your journey and learn to say goodbye to those that don't. You cannot be held back from your calling, which gives you the most peace and comfort in life, for if you do, you will go through life not enjoying it at all. When you are brave enough to learn that things aren't right when you understand that your pathway will have many twists and turns and these changes will sometimes be necessary for the good of all. When you try to control a situation to make it the way you want or what you think it should be, you must make that leap; you have to cut your cords and move on. Your future, which you are yet to witness, may surprise you, and later present itself to you in a way that you will later understand, why certain events on your journey had to happen. Look forward to your future, go with the flow and stop trying to control things. If you give into your ego, you give into the assumption that life is a better experience by predicting the outcome. Instead, start to enjoy life and everything it has to offer.

Meditation Five: Surrendering

We live in a world where we love to control our lives. We think it makes us feel safe and secure to have a better understanding of how our day will plan out. Holding on tightly to our thoughts and ideas, we manipulate outcomes and make sure things happen. But controlling our lives restricts the possibilities of what can happen when we loosen our grip.

Does being out of control make you fearful? Does this make heart beat faster? Does it make chest tighten?

If you put yourself in an unknown situation, where anything could happen, would you forever judge yourself on the outcome? Does your mind think about what you need to happen rather than what will? For you see control is a rooted fear.

Whenever we let go, we move into a 'flow,' and without realising it, life will become easier. More space is created for wonderful possibilities that maybe we never thought could happen. When you are faced with a situation, listen to your inner voice that you will be okay no matter what circumstances come your way.

You have probably heard the saying "go with the flow," and that's what you need to do here. Surrender your mind to the erratic behaviour, that the controlled mind has created, calm the breath and heart rate will also slow. Ironically by trying to control things you have less control.

In your mind gently say this mantra: I choose to surrender now. I am calm I am peaceful, I choose to let go. Repeat mantra.

Lifelong Learning

Learning never stops. Never think it's time to hang up your boots as you've learnt as much as you need to. You will carry on learning from the day you were born until the day you die. In some stages of your life, you will learn at a much faster pace than others. The things you learn will inspire you and motivate you. At other stages your learning may seem tiresome and tedious, and the lessons will take more time to absorb. Don't let this put you off learning, as everything you learn will be useful to you at some point; even if the reasons don't seem apparent now. Learning, however, is so much easier when you enjoy it and have support and encouragement along the way, although sometimes a lack of support can make you more determined to succeed.

When I was growing up and attending high school, I wasn't very interested in learning. I was enjoying life and all the fun that goes with it. I didn't want to sit in a room in silence and study. I sat listening to my music, sometimes even watching the television at the same time as trying to study. I never found myself to be one of the brighter kids at school, as some would brand themselves. I was interested in life, health, and fitness, even though I abused my body by starving myself at times and exercising beyond what my body needed in a day. I didn't want to be stuck at home; I wanted to be outside and enjoying nature, I wanted to cycle everywhere to feel the wind in my hair. I became obsessed with fitness, cycling, muscle building, slimming, Judo, Squash, Sea Cadets and my boyfriend. I even managed to squeeze in some work as well. At the time I thought this was having a good effect on me. I had not come across the concept of moderation, although this is the key to a healthy, happy and balanced life. There came a point where I couldn't continue the rollercoaster ride without it hurting my day to day life.

I soon struggled to get up in the morning. In the end, my Dad (my grandfather who raised me like a father) put an intercom in my room and would call me on it every morning, several times in fact, as I was too cosy in my bed to start the day early. I often turned up at school late, missing lessons to go for a cycle ride, sometimes alone and sometimes with one of my friends, and learning seemed so far away from what I wanted to do.

My body started to become fragile from where I skipped meals and was becoming starved of the important vitamins and nutrients it so needed. Some of my teeth started to crack from the lack of calcium in my diet and as they were my adult teeth some now only have the fronts. I fractured my collarbone in Judo twice in succession. Where I had skipped meals, I often got stomach cramps, through an obsession with being thin like models in magazines, competing with my friends and trying to be something that deep down I did not like.

My Dad would say to me, "Make something of yourself, leave boys alone, you don't want to be dyslexic like me with no papers;" (meaning he had no certificates). But although I respected my Dad, as he was a very influential person in my life, I was growing up, and I wanted to learn my way, which inevitably was the hard way. So, I ignored him and started pushing the boundaries. I would stay out, not caring about how my parents felt, or how much they worried about where I was. I was becoming a typical rebellious teenager, and I didn't want to be around my parents. I left school with some GCSEs but not as many as I could have achieved had I put in even half the effort into my school life, as I did in my social life.

Where did all this leave me? Well, I did have a part-time job whilst at school, so I continued to work part time and decided to go to college and resit two of my exams and study a few new subjects, as there were so many more options available at college compared to school. I still enjoyed my social life and boys, and soon I started drinking. I would go from one obsession to another. Maybe you can relate to this. But I had still not grasped that too much of a 'good thing' can turn out to be bad.

I left the job I had as one with better pay became available and would be perfect to work around my holidays prior to starting college. So, I took on a part-time position selling ice cream. The business was run by two men in their early twenties, and I instantly took a liking to the man that had interviewed me as did he to me. He was a white male with a large back and had brown wavy hair, he was my type. He came across as very charming and witty. The two owners seemed to be doing well with all the different sites that their ice cream vans and trailers were distributed across and the team they employed. I would be called into work as and when needed. I would get a cab or bus to the office each time, and then the owner would drive me in his car to the various sites, spread across Broadstairs, Grove Ferry, Sandwich, and Deal.

On my first day at work, we had driven back to the office and whilst still in the car chatting, a woman in a jeep came driving straight towards us at an alarming speed. The owner said something to try and dismiss what had occurred and quickly sent me on my way home, whilst he got out to talk to the woman. I never asked who she was nor, did he tell me, but she was clearly very upset with him about something. With the look in her eyes, when she stopped the car, she seemed more than a business acquaintance.

Over the course of time, my boss and I started to mix business with pleasure, and we soon became an item. He was quite a drinker though, and we would sometimes have a few drinks after work, but never needed to go far as his office filing cabinet was filled with booze rather than files. Sometimes when he ran out, we would pop out to the newsagent and buy another bottle of vodka or two. We would end our evenings drinking, and I would often go home when he had fallen asleep from tiredness and too much alcohol.

My boss was the type of person who enjoyed putting me down. He would often say how fat I was, although I was only a size eight at the time. He would squeeze my stomach and say how big I was getting. So, I started to think about what he was saying. I thought about how easy it had been to eat less before, so I could do this again now. I started to skip meals again, but the amount of drink I consumed increased considerably. If you have ever been in a relationship with an alcoholic, you know how easy this can be, if you have little self-control. I started to notice how I would crave a drink instead of food and how, in the mornings, I wanted a stiff drink. I would go out drinking with my friends to the nightclubs at least twice a week. Alcohol was so cheap; in fact, the soft drinks were dearer, so it seemed to make sense to me at the time to have a Vodka or a Rum with Coke, rather than the latter on its own. I rarely mixed my drinks, so hangovers weren't something I got very often, and the more I drank, the less they occurred. What I did notice though were the awful pains I started to get in my stomach. It was so bad I had stomach cramps for hours on end. It was a sign that my body was telling me to slow down and take more care of my body. I didn't take any notice at first though, as I was young, not even officially an adult. I was enjoying this man and his behaviour, but now it was having a negative effect on me, which I seemed oblivious to.

As I continued to work for the company there came a time when my boss asked if he could pay my wages a day later, when normally, I'd get paid on the day that I worked. I didn't mind and said this was fine. Then he did it the next time and the next. One day I turned up to work, and he took me to the Broadstairs site. When the ice cream delivery arrived, he said he had no money to pay for it. I offered to get some money from the bank and pay, on the basis that he paid me back that day. So, here I was offering to pay my boss's bill for his stock. I walked up to the bank and withdrew the £200 he needed and loaned him the money. Later that day he gave me the money for the delivery but said he still didn't have enough to pay my wages. At this stage, I was starting to get a little fed up with not being paid for work. My family also started to ask questions about him but I gave them limited amount of information, however even based on the little I told them they still took a disliking to him and his behaviour.

I was now growing up very fast and wanted to move on with my life, so I decided to move out of my grandparents and into my Mums. Mum was looking forward to me moving in, and I found it exciting at first. It was quite a change for me as I was used to living at home and being waited on, now though things would be very different. My Mum wasn't around very much, as I had expected her to be and often went away on weekends with her partner. But I soon got used to it.

One day my boss asked me to work for his uncle in Romford, about 80 miles away from where I lived. He needed me to help manage his market stall for the day. I didn't want to go and did it as a favour for him. I had to get to where my boss lived, where he shared a room with his mate at his Mum's house. It was early in the morning, probably around 4am. He then dropped me off at his uncle's place in a different part of Ramsgate. I had dressed warmly as it was cold. His uncle wasn't quite ready to go, so I stayed and had a brief chat with his uncle's girlfriend before we set off.

It was strange working on a market stall. We had to set it up and then I had to tout for business from the passing public, trying to convince people to buy things. It was not something that flowed easily for me. We also met a fellow stall holder, and my boss's uncle wanted to buy all his army surplus stock, to sell on the stall. They agreed on the price, but we still needed to sell a fair bit to raise the all money needed. I was standing in the cold and freezing so I was offered a long-sleeved army top, hat and gloves by the other stall holder and I soon warmed-up a little. As the day unfolded, having been there for several hours, it turned out that my boss's uncle was going out afterward and not back home to Ramsgate. So here I was, miles away from home with no money or any form of transport. My boss's uncle asked the chap with the army clothes to give me a lift back home. It looked like I had no choice and had to take the lift. We chatted on the way back, although I felt very uncomfortable in his company and even more so when we got nearer to my Mum's house, as he said he needed the toilet and asked if he could use mine. I had already said that my mother was not home and now he was asking to use the toilet. This started to play on my mind, and I tried not to show that I was feeling unhappy and uncomfortable about this. When we arrived outside my Mum's house, I said, "I don't think Mum would like you using her toilet, but there are plenty of toilets near the Clock Tower, if you head towards the seafront on your way back you will find one to use," I thanked him for the lift and let myself in with a sigh of relief, that not only had I got back, but no harm had come to me.

My boss now owed me for this work as well and seemed to be avoiding paying me. I eventually started to become aware of how he was taking advantage of my good nature.

I got home from college one day, and no one was there, which was often the case, so I thought I'd cook pie, potatoes, and vegetables for dinner. I went into the kitchen and picked up a tin opener to open the tinned pie and sliced my finger on the tin so badly that it would not stop bleeding, no matter what I tried. I held it up and put plasters on, but still, it bled. The only option left was going to the hospital. I phoned my boss, who said he would meet me at the hospital as soon as he could. As I was getting ready to walk to the local accident and emergency, Mum came home and seeing what I had done, walked with me to the hospital. I had a little joke with her that I could not go inside until I had my lipstick on and soon I found some in my pocket, so I was on my way. I walked in, and the nurse said she would clean and apply butterfly stitches to the cut stop it bleeding. They finished it with a bandage dressing, which seemed to help. My boss eventually turned up on our way out and gave us a lift back and said he couldn't stop but would come over later. Mum took an instant disliking to him and told me that she did not want him in the house. When I later told him he understandably took offence to this.

The next day whilst I was at college; he posted a photo of me, which I had given him, through my letterbox—he had ripped it to shreds. My stepfather found it and said I should make sure my mother didn't see it. It seemed rather petty at the time but probably made my boyfriend feel better.

Work had slowed down, and he was not contacting me to meet him as much as before. I had now started college and travelled in by train. On the train one day, I sat opposite a girl I knew from school. She asked how things were going, as she knew I was seeing him and said, "You know he's been sleeping with his cousin don't you?" I was taken aback as I knew his 1st cousin quite well having been to school with her. I was surprised and angry at the same time. I realised now that I had to find a way to get my wages paid, as he probably didn't intend to pay me.

I made an appointment to see a solicitor, and fortunately, back then legal aid was available. I told the solicitor that my boss owed me over £400 and that I was dating him. He was understanding towards me and appreciated that at sixteen years of age I was quite a naïve young lady, who had got herself into a situation and needed proper advice and support. He rang my boss who seemed to ignore his calls until he wrote to him and finally got a response. The solicitor informed me that my boss wanted to personally speak to me to try and resolve this and asked me what I thought.

I went to see my boss, and he said that he knew he owed me money but he had financial problems and would pay me back, but was not sure when that would be. He therefore wanted to know if could I let the work I did for his uncle 'slide', as it was his uncle that should have paid me and not him. I said "okay" as I wanted to be paid something so that we could get this matter resolved.

Over the coming weeks, I still hadn't been paid so decided to go back to the solicitor. The solicitor wrote again to him, advising that if he did not pay me the matter would have to be dealt with, in a small claims court. Up until then, I guess he thought he had me spinning around his little finger, and for a while he did.

He rang me one night to speak to me on the landline, and my stepfather handed me the phone. My stepfather soon got irritated by this as he was trying to watch the TV but the only phone we had was in the same room, so he couldn't hear properly. My boss soon rang again, and I spoke to him, whilst he talked about nonsense. His constant ringing continued. He was clearly drunk and was trying to make small talk. My stepfather by now was very annoyed and told him to stop ringing, but still, he didn't listen. In the end, I told my stepfather that I'd go to his flat, he was now renting with his friend which was around twenty minutes' walk away.

He couldn't understand what he was doing wrong by phoning me, even though it was late at night. He had his hands all over me and I kept telling him to 'get off,' but he wouldn't listen, he started to undress himself and me as he took me into the next room, where I tried to talk to him, and again he wouldn't leave me alone. I pushed him off the best I could as I reminded him that I needed to go home as I had college in the morning. I finally managed to force him off me, which I probably only managed as he was so drunk. I made my way home alone in the dark, as quickly as I could. The next day my stepfather wanted to know what had happened and I said, "That's it, I have finished with him now."

I made another visit to the solicitor who told me that he had heard from my boss who said he owed me less, as he had deducted the day that I worked for his uncle. Although I felt that I shouldn't let him, I wanted to get on with my life, and so I agreed on the amount he stated. Still trying to have the upper hand, he decided to make the payment as three cheques to be cashed over a three-month period. I told the solicitor. "That's fine" and took the cheques. The solicitor informed me that if any of the cheques bounced I would need to proceed with a small claims case, but luckily, that didn't happen. In hindsight, I should have seen that this man was trouble on my first day at work when I saw that woman in the high-speed car incident.

A couple of weeks later I met someone else; he seemed nice enough and quiet at times. We were opposites in many ways. He was tall, white skinned with blonde hair, had no interest in learning to drive, whilst I was looking forward to the freedom that driving a car would offer. We walked almost everywhere, which was quite hard to do in the beginning with his long legs and my short ones, but I soon learnt to walk faster, and I started to enjoy the fresh air. It was clear early on that he lacked the drive to do anything further with his life. There was always something that prevented him from moving on and getting a job. Once he refused to wash his boss's car, and was sacked. Then there was the time he went to an interview but never went in, as the owners had an Alsatian and he was afraid of dogs. Most of the time he seemed to live in a dream world. I suggested he went back to college, having first met him there when we both attended the same drama course in which he played the character as my husband, but the college soon dismissed him for missing lessons and talking back to the tutor.

He lacked the enthusiasm to work and was no longer interested in educating himself anymore. The only thing that interested him was music and writing songs. He wrote songs about me on several occasions as well as other things but left them to gather dust. I started to get bored with our relationship, thinking there must be more to a happy relationship than this. I spoke to my Mum as she seemed happy in her relationship at the time and told her how unhappy I felt. She thought ending it would be a bad idea as she said I had already gone to bed with this man and people may start to brand me a slag. This wasn't what I wanted to hear as it did not support my decision, and made me feel that I should probably rethink, whether I wanted to make it work. Although only sixteen I had to make some grown up decisions.

I was staying at my grandparents' house one day, which I did once a week, after moving out soon after I had left high school. My boyfriend came to visit me, for a couple of hours. On this occasion, he said that his ribs were hurting. I asked him why and he said he got into a fight over me, at the nightclub. He told me that someone he knew had called me a slag. I was quite taken aback by this, firstly because I could not understand why someone would think that, aside from my mother's previous comments and secondly, why he would get into a fight as he never seemed the type to fight, it was very out of character. Anyway, I went downstairs and asked one of my aunts for a cold flannel; she asked why, and I told her that my boyfriend had been in a fight outside the nightclub over the weekend and was bruised. She said, "That was not very nice," and gave me a flannel and arnica to put on it. I gave it to him to try and help him where I could, although I must admit I could not see any visible signs of bruises or marks, so I assumed it must have been internal. I didn't own a mobile phone then and was therefore reliant on the landline, so was not accustomed to speaking to him every day. I did what I could and felt sorry for him but was surprised about what he said had happened.

It was early days in our relationship, and I still felt like ending it, but never seemed to find the right moment. My feelings towards him did increase as the weeks passed. I found this tended to happen the more I spent time with someone at the beginning of a relationship. One day my boyfriend said he had a surprise for me and wanted me to get a taxi to his home the following weekend. He had spoken to me previously about how his brothers had all got engaged or were now married and he was the last one left, so I had an inclination that he was going to ask me to marry him. I spoke to my friends and my Mum and apart from him possibly buying me a kitten we were all coming to similar conclusions. So, a week later I went to his parent's home where he lived. It took him a while, but he eventually came out and asked me to marry him whilst presenting me with an engagement ring. I had already decided what I was going to say before he had asked me. I think my answer was based on being young and to the thought of being engaged for the first time, which predominantly was why I said yes. All the thoughts in the week preceding and following, were no longer about not being with him, but about how excited I was and feeling special. Once I said yes, my head started thinking about who I should tell first and where our wedding would be and all the planning we had to do. I felt pleased with my decision and how exciting it was to have a wedding to look forward to, I told my family first, then my friends. Some of my friends and family took it quite badly; they thought I was mad to be thinking of getting married at seventeen.

My anticipation and dreams of being married started to take over, affecting my ego. But in that whirlwind moment, I got carried away. The sense of excitement and joy of becoming the first from my school year to be married and being married before my mother as she had never married but cohabitated with her partner of eleven years. It was going to my head so much that I was forgetting the actual reason for getting married in the first place—to spend the rest of my life with my partner.

It was not long before we set a date for the wedding, which was to be held the following year. This would give us time to save, plan, and for me to reach eighteen, to make the wedding legal in England. Less than a month passed, Mum seemed a little jealous and spoke to my stepfather about how weird it would be for her daughter to be married before her. So, she soon announced that she too was getting married, but that they were going to get married this year. I felt like after all this time they spent together they wouldn't have even thought about getting married, had I not told them my plans, but still, I was happy for them.

My fiancée and I enjoyed each other's company to a point, doing things young people do. We decided to set up home together. We stayed in the flat most of the time playing computer games or listening to our vinyl's, and we even got a kitten whom I named Gizmo. She was so cute, I saw her as my baby. I continued with my GCSEs, but problems in my personal life started to occur with my fiancée. Things happened that hurt and seemed quite unforgiveable on my part and being young I was not sure if we could reach into our hearts to find ways to solve them when all I could think was; this is how it would always be.

I didn't drink alcohol anymore apart from the odd occasion, and I was not interested in exercising like I used to. Even though the unhappiness in my life was starting to increase, I seemed settled in some ways, and I think this was the reason I stayed. As more weeks passed other things happened in our relationship and it felt like it was going to be more and more difficult to repair, I decided it would be best to separate to see how things went.

We kept in daily contact either by phone, meeting at Mums, or at the park and so forth and this made the whole separation so much harder. We talked about our feelings and decided to continue to get married and give it a go to see where it would lead. By now my kitten was six months and was pregnant. I saw her giving birth, which to me was one of the most amazing things I had ever witnessed at a young age. She even let me handle the kittens, which was quite unusual, as often if a cat smells human scent on her kittens they tend to reject them. One by one I placed them in a warm cardboard box with a blanket inside and even though they all turned out to be female we decided to name them Nermal, Da-Niro, and Garfield. They were so sweet and were with me every day making funny squealing noises as they lay next to me in my bed. Each day they would rush over to me when I got up. When people heard that I had all the kittens they all wanted one. However, I got attached to them very early on even though it wasn't the ideal situation. Living in a small bedroom at my Mums, with a cat and three kittens worked for me and I enjoyed their company, although I had not thought about how I was going to afford to look after them.

Our wedding day came, and we planned it the best we could. Family helped out with costs as at eighteen years old I didn't have a lot of money to scrape together. My Dad bought my dress, and my Mum and step-father paid for the hall hire. My soon to be father-in-law took on the role of the chauffeur and took us to and from the registry office. On our wedding day, the registrar forgot to tell us to kiss to seal the marriage, which gave me an odd feeling about this day of celebration.

Despite this, our day seemed to be going well. We had a few hours before the evening reception, and I wanted to go back home to change my clothes, so my father-in-law drove my husband and I over to my Mum's. I rushed up the stairs opened my bedroom door, and the kittens came running over to me, but as they did, I accidentally stood on Garfield with my stiletto shoes and perforated her lungs. I felt mortified about what had happened and had to convince my father-in-law to take her to a Vet, as neither he nor my new husband could see the point in this, but I was not prepared to leave her there to suffer not knowing the outcome. After this I did not want to go to the reception, I saw this as the second sign that things were wrong with the marriage, for this to happen on the very first day of our wedding, but my family were looking forward to the gathering and convinced me to go.

I finally picked myself up, the best I could and wiped away the tears, putting on a fresh layer of makeup. After the ordeal with the kitten earlier, I decided to stay at my husband's home for the night, as I didn't want to go back home, but we had spent all our money on food and drink and couldn't afford a cab. No one seemed forthcoming in offering us a lift and most were going in completely different directions or already had a car full of people, and I didn't like to ask for money on a day where people had already bought us gifts. So, the reality of this amazing wedding had not gone how I expected and would finish off with us walking back nearly three miles in the cold and dark.

The next day I was told that the kitten had died, I was upset and decided that I would somehow find a way to keep the remaining kittens as I did not want anyone else to have them. I had that distraught feeling when you lose a pet that I should have been more careful when entering my bedroom as they were so tiny, but unfortunately in that moment of haste one had died.

Over time my husband and I decided we again needed to find a place of our own to set up home. A few months passed before we found somewhere around the corner from my Mums and thought this would be ideal for us. Two weeks into the new house we were sitting on our beds watching TV when an image of a cat came to the window. This was most unusual as it looked like my cat Gizzmo, yet we were one storey up so there was no way my cat would go up there, but somehow, I knew it was her. She wasn't her full colour but more of a hazy white. With logic trying to take precedence it seemed impossible that this could be her. I told my husband what I had seen, and he dismissed what I said, as implausible. About ten minutes later we heard a knock at the door, and my husband went down the stairs to see who it was. He found the next door neighbour there and she had come to tell us that she had found one of our cat's dead on the road. Someone must have knocked her down and killed her. My husband shut the door and came and told me, as all the cats were outside I rushed down and started to call them in. One by one they approached me; Da-Niro then Nermal and that was it, I knew then that what I had seen at the window was the image of my now deceased cat.

So here we were again only two weeks into our new home, and I was facing more devastating news. I wasn't sure where my life was going at this stage, my husband did not work, and I was on a training course, learning Administration, although I found I lacked any motivation for it. I wanted to do something.

The weeks passed, and I was sitting in the front room reading an advert in a magazine about Tarot reading and decided to give it a try. My great Nan Annie, used to read tea leaves before I was born, but my maternal Nan was against this, being religious. With the television portrayal of Tarot reading as a non-Christian activity, it was regarded as some kind of dark magic that would be of no benefit and was not to be messed with. However, I was always intrigued by how it worked, so I decided to ring the advert. A woman answered to ask if I would like a recording, which I thought would be a good idea.

She spoke about many things and so much of it I could relate to, even though she didn't know anything personal about me, apart from my name and that I had confirmed to her that I was over eighteen to make the call. She said you had a celebration of some kind and that would now be over. The only thing that came to my mind was the possibility that she was referring to my marriage and now it had probably served its purpose, and it was time to move on. She also spoke about education and said I would be in education for a very long time, although at the time I dismissed this as I could not see myself doing that. She spoke about a new man coming into my life, which would be a lot older than me but would want something back in return. She spoke about something that had upset me, which brought the death of my cat to the forefront of my mind. I decided to take heed of what she had said, as it seemed the accuracy of what was being said outweighed anything that I did not understand or ring true at that moment.

Surprises Aren't Always Nice

At home one day I walked to the front door and saw what the postman had brought, and amongst the mail was a letter from the estate agents whom we rented the house from, addressed to both my husband and I. It stated that we had fallen behind on the rent. I thought this could not be the case as I mainly dealt with the money, as before our marriage my fiancée had taken some of our money meant for bills and spent it on wrestling videos without even telling me. So, I was a little surprised to see this letter, hoping that he hadn't done anything of a similar nature, although my intuition was telling me he had. I asked my husband for the receipts for all the payments he had made, only to find that many were missing or as the case started to unfold, never existed, hence the reason for the letter. I tried in vain to correct this with extra payments, but the owners of the house decided at that point to sell the house. I made sure we got together all the money to cover what was owed but it was too late—they served us with eviction papers, giving us two weeks to find somewhere else to live.

We found a flat to rent with another estate agent and handed over our £200 deposit. We packed, ready to move and ordered the removal van. However, on the day we were moving the estate agents would not give us the keys, saying we had not disclosed that we were being evicted. All money we had owed was paid, and we did not see how this was now important, but the estate agent decided he was now going to keep the deposit as an admin fee and refused to rent the flat to us. I phoned the estate agents we were previously with explaining that we were unable to move and needed to stay a bit longer until we found another suitable place; otherwise we would be homeless. As we had repaid the overdue rent, they agreed that this would be acceptable for a short period.

Still, some things happen for a reason, and this taught me to be more careful about whom to trust. The house wasn't in a good condition and we had previously contacted the council about the poor living conditions and high levels of damp causing mould and fungi to grow. The damp never dried out as there was only a single coal fire to heat the house, which was never adequate, especially when the coal ran out. We would spend most of our evenings sitting in the bed upstairs as it always seemed warmer up there. We decided our next option was to contact the council again to try and get help to find another home. They proved to be more helpful than I thought they would be and found us a studio flat through a private landlord, which was perfect for us.

Going back, to when I was living in the house, I had flicked through the local paper and come across a Sports course. It seemed like something I would be interested in, having undertaken many types of sports and exercise before. I did, however, notice that they wanted applicants to carry out a fitness test before acceptance on the course. Having not exercised for some time, I assumed I would fail and decided not to enrol, but remembering to the voice of the woman who had read my tarot about education, I thought something else would come up.

Continuing through the papers I stumbled upon another course, on Holistic Therapy, learning about Reflexology and Aromatherapy. I already knew that Aromatherapy creates wonderful smells and has many benefits but not much more beyond this. So, I enrolled on the course and felt pleased with my decision when I was accepted. This was where my spiritual journey began.

At college, I enjoyed what I was learning. In fact, I found it was not only fun and interesting, but learning came easily. It seemed much easier than anything I had done before. And why was that? Well, it seemed that I now understood that I was a visual learner. Not only was I able to relate to this type of learning but I also started to grasp the concepts quickly, through what I was being shown. I was no longer predominately taught from a book, where sometimes I would struggle to read, and would often have to re-read the same thing before it would register in my brain. I was I no longer surrounded with high school learners whose interests were scattered. I was now in a class-room environment surrounded by like minded students, learning about something that not only interested me, but that could help others. When I did help others, I enjoyed it and felt rewarded at the same time. I finally felt like I found somewhere I belonged.

Growing Older

By the time I reached twenty-one, in the first year of studying my new course, my Dad had become very ill with incurable cancer. It was a hard time for my family and I, to see someone suffering in pain and not be able to help or improve his condition.

Some people may say it is easier if you know that someone is dying, at least you have time to deal with it. Well, that's not always the case. In my situation, the man I saw as my father for my entire life was deteriorating, far quicker than

I or anyone had thought—wasting away, minute by minute, hour by hour and day by day. The time we had left with him seemed to be slipping away so quickly; it was as if time had suddenly sped up and no matter how much we tried it was not slowing down.

At the same time that my Dad was going through his ordeal, my marriage had gone stagnant. We were more like friends than anything else. My husband still had no interest in working, but some would say he was a good homemaker. A homemaker, however, was not want I needed; I needed someone with ambition in life, someone with drive, who saw life as part of the goal but not as the end goal. I'd go home from studying five days a week to talk solely about how my day had been, only for my husband to have nothing to talk about or very little of interest to say. I thought about our marriage for some time, before I managed to pick up the courage to tell him that I was unhappy and that things needed to change for it to improve, but still, I thought the end of our marriage would be inevitable.

In the meantime, I started to become friendly with an older man from college who at the time was fourteen years my senior. He seemed helpful at times and would ask me out, so that I wasn't staring at four walls most of the weekend, which was how I was feeling with my husband at the time. I started to enjoy this man's company far more than I did my husband, and I seemed to be spending more time with my friends than I had in a long time, which I also enjoyed. I found this man interesting, and he started to take an interest in me more and more.

I was craving attention and love, all of which I felt my marriage lacked. As I started to see what my marriage was lacking, I became convinced that my marriage had served its time and that there was nothing more that I could add to it to improve it, it was now time to call it an end. I spoke with my family about this; I told them how I felt and that there was someone else that had started to make me feel happy and alive again. They felt that I should move on and not let this marriage that I had been in for a few years now, hold me back anymore. I was surprised by their thoughts, but also pleased that they were supporting my decision. My grandparents had been very anti-divorce before this point, having been married themselves for forty-eight years, but I think they could see I was unhappy. It was a difficult decision calling an end to a marriage, but nothing improved, and so I felt it had to be done. I soon started to date the chap I had met at college, hoping that my life would be better now.

Dad Was Unwell

Dad's health continued to deteriorate to the point of him going to a Hospice, and this now seemed like it would be the last place his soul would be. At this point in my life, stress started to affect me quite badly. Not only was Dad in the local Hospice, but I had ended my marriage, and now my coursework was due imminently. All the important things to me seemed to be piling up. Then I caught a cold, which progressed to bronchitis. But it didn't stop there; as I also developed shingles, which made it almost impossible for me to talk. The shingles were scattered across my entire body including the inside my throat. I knew I shouldn't have gone to the Hospice with Dad being so ill, but I needed to go, and it seemed likely if it was going to be the last time I would see him. So regardless of how I felt, I dosed myself up with antibiotics and applied calamine lotion to stop the scratching. The bronchitis made me lethargic, but I wanted to see Dad, and that is what I did. You see when you are given an opportunity to see someone in what maybe their final hours you would understand why I had to go.

I visited Dad on several occasions at the Hospice before and this time was no different with him lying there in bed.

It had now reached the point where the doctors and nurses decided to take Dad off the drip that was feeding him, as his body was rejecting all types of food. They also removed the morphine drip, he was given to help curb the pain. They felt at this stage there was not much more they could do. I sat and talked to him for a while and he said he could see his brother, Tom, although his brother had died of Leukaemia about six months earlier. He followed this by saying that he could see a bright light with a tunnel at the end and that he could see his daughter, Trudy, although he had six daughters Trudy had died when she was eleven years old from kidney disease. He said he felt that they were talking to him and asking him if he was ready.

We continued to talk and discussed that, if he wanted to, he could reach them and go, but I don't think he was quite ready at that moment. Instead, he held out until the next morning. He was lying in his bed and didn't have the energy to talk to anyone during his visit from his wife (my Nan) and daughter. They said they stayed for a while, but he laid there and said nothing, so after a period of time they thought it was best to leave. As they were leaving, almost at the door, the nurses called them back to say that Maurice had let out a sigh and with that Dad had died. Despite all the pain and suffering, he must have gone through, it was nice to hear that he had two of the people he loved near his side when he passed.

I was at college on the day and heard the tragic news. I had to sit down as I took it in. It was a sad day, and my boyfriend who attended the same college came to comfort me. The tutors told him to take me home. We went back to his flat, and he suggested that we should go for a walk. We went out for a bit, but my tears did not flow. My boyfriend started to act differently from how he normally was, his behaviour towards me had changed. He said in a very unsympathetic voice, "Well aren't you going to cry then", I replied, "Well, I will when I can, but it's hard at the moment", for I was not going to force the tears, they were stuck, and a feeling of shock had come over me.

Several days had passed before I cried properly and when I did it was like a waterfall pouring over a cliff, and it was difficult to stop. By this time, I was spending more and more time with my boyfriend, however in contrast to what he had previously said, he now complained about me crying, telling me to stop—as if I had control over when I could and couldn't cry. His behaviour at the time seemed absurd and not comforting in any way, given the situation, but I dismissed this, as I already had far too much to deal with. Despite his irrational behaviour, I went with this world wind romance and when shortly after he asked if I wanted to move in with him, I agreed as I felt somewhere fresh was what I needed.

I moved from the flat I had been living in with my husband to the new flat that my boyfriend and I took a lease on to set up home, thinking this would be the change I needed.

There would be times that I would go over what Dad had previously said to me, about getting myself an education, and I decided now was the time to honour this, so I threw myself into it with open arms. I filed to divorce my husband, which didn't take long as we had grown apart, had no children and split everything else we owned.

Days with my boyfriend were unsettled at times. I was at home on one occasion, having made dinner and sat down to study for an exam, which I had to take the next day. My boyfriend came in with his friend and asked me to iron his shirt as he was going out to a stag party that evening. I didn't want to drop my studies there and then as he was quite capable of ironing his shirt, so I told him no. He stormed off with his friend insulting me about how lazy I was and then only answered my phone calls with a rant. He went to the stag party and was supposed to go to work afterwards; he didn't go but instead stayed out until the early hours of the morning and blamed me that he didn't go to work.

My boyfriend used to work on weekends only on evening shifts. On one occasion a friend popped in to see us as he was staying with family for a few days. After we sat talking for a while, my boyfriend said to his friend, "Are you going off to see your Mum now, as I need to go to work?", his friend replied, "No, I'll spend some time talking to Donella if that's okay", He said, "Okay", and went off to work. We chatted a bit longer, mainly about my boyfriend. I was getting tired, so I said, "You'll have to go as I need to go to bed." We bid our goodbyes, and off he went.

The next day was Saturday and all three of us had planned to go out that night. I spent the morning out with a girlfriend and bought myself a plain, inexpensive black dress, which was not as conservative as some of my other clothes. When I got dressed in the evening and walked downstairs, ready to go out, my boyfriend remarked, "I hope you are not wearing that out," to which I replied, "Yes, I am, why?" He said, "It's not your normal type of dress, go and change it." I said, "No, I only bought it today, and I can't see anything wrong with it apart from it being slightly shorter than others that I have." This remark made him angry.

His friend arrived at this point, and so he let it slip, and we set off in his friend's car heading for a local nightclub. When we got there his friend asked if I liked dancing. I replied "Yes". He asked, "If I speak to your boyfriend can we all go and dance to the next song?" I said, "Yes that's fine". When my boyfriend came over he said, "Why have you agreed to dance with him?" I asked, "What?" He repeated, "Why are you going to dance with him?" I stated, "That's not what I said or meant, I meant we will all dance on the floor together", he said. "That's not what he thinks", I insisted, "Well that's what I meant". With that he said, "When he comes back tell him you are not dancing". So, I did as he asked, not to cause any more fuss.

We went to the next nightclub and walked up the stairs to the dance floor. After a drink I needed the ladies room and said, "I'll be back soon." I went off, and when I got out, my boyfriend was waiting outside. He grabbed me forcefully by my arm and asked, "Where have you been?" I told him, "In the toilet, you know that." He said, "My mate also went to the toilet after you so is he in there as well?" I said, "No of course not, there are other women in there." He said whilst still holding tightly to my arm, "Right, I am going to take you over to the dance floor now, and we can dance together." I said, "I don't want to dance now." He said, "So you'll dance with him, but you won't dance with me. That's it, Donella, I've had enough, you are a whore and have been sleeping with him, I want you to go to the flat, get all your stuff and move out."

I was extremely hurt, embarrassed and upset by what he had said. He accused me of something I had not done. He humiliated and shouted at me in front of hordes of people and told me to move out. It was early in the morning and I had nowhere to go. I ran down the stairs crying my eyes out, running across the road to the beach opposite, to drown my sorrows.

His mate had come out of the men's toilets by now and seen the last part of the argument. He followed my boyfriend downstairs and went to get the car. My boyfriend followed me across the road, and when he caught up with me, told me to go home with him and that his mate had gone to get the car. I was so confused about what he wanted me to do and what he didn't, but it was late and cold and so I agreed to get into the car. I got in and his mate dropped us home.

My boyfriend continued his accusations that he thought I was sleeping with his friend; I told him I wasn't. He explained that he got angry, and that I should not say anything about it to his friend when he visited the next day. The whole ridiculous scenario was created in his head and now he wanted me to pretend as if nothing had happened and so, foolish as I was back then, I did exactly that.

Time passed, and my divorce came through, so my boyfriend and I got married, whilst I was still the tender age of twenty-one. But being married did not mean that the problems got better, in fact, they got a whole lot worse. In my naivety I thought marriage, had changed him, and what I thought were teething problems in the beginning, now erupted to something much uglier. He now started to show his true colours. It was as if this man now owned me, I was his property, and I had to do what he wanted me to do, otherwise life would be worse than what it was. I withdrew into myself and from others. When we were around other people he would say "she's shy, she doesn't speak much". He said this so often, that eventually, that is what I became. I fed into his way of thinking and manipulative behaviour.

My husband and I argued a lot. I cannot remember any given month where we didn't. Life was not what I hoped it would be. It was like jumping from the frying pan straight into the fire. I did not know what to do and felt that I had nowhere else to turn, so I did the only thing I felt I could at the time, and stayed put, trying to focus on going forward with my learning. I went on with my studies and completed my holistic therapy course and soon started offering treatments to clients in a salon. But I needed to grow the business and learn more, so I decided to undertake a beauty therapy course at my local college, and managed to complete it in one year. This had never been done before due to the amount of work learners were expected to do, but I kept going and completed the course and was awarded student of the year.

At the age of twenty-two, I set up a Beauty and Holistic business by opening a salon. I offered treatments that I studied at college and with other training providers. Running my business made me feel alive again, as it was about showing the world that I was somehow still a woman, even though my husband was making me feel like a scared little girl.

The salon was ticking over with its two beauty rooms, nail bar, tanning cubicle and steam capsule. However, there were moments when I felt it was hard going, working to pay off rent, loans and hire purchases accumulated from running a business. Sometimes I would wonder if life would get any easier.

Then disaster broke out when a fire damaged the electrical circuits. I spent a year and a half building my salon from scratch and now I had Health and Safety inspectors imposing a requirement for a safety certificate on the entire property, which included the three bedroom flat above, where I lived. The repair costs ran into thousands, and with other costs to factor in, I was having to make quick decisions. It became worse when I found out that the insurance company had refused to pay out, as they considered having electricity even though unsafe would still be fine to run my business on, but it was not. The total cost was beyond what I could afford to pay and I stood to lose it all. I approached the landlord who shunned his responsibility, stating he could help, but only as far as sending a non-qualified electrician to cap off the faulty wires and not rewire the building, which was the health and safety requirement to pass the building off and get my business up and running again.

I was left with no choice but to close my business down and lose all I had worked for. I closed the shop almost immediately after this, not having time to let my existing clients know. My attention now was focussed on finding somewhere for my husband and I to live.

I am sure many of you can relate to that feeling of trying to achieve something only to be pushed back. Despite this, my work felt to me like it was my only way of going forward and going forward is what I intended to do.

Once I managed to find somewhere for us to live the next step was to think about how I could adapt my business to work with the clients I had left. I set up a mobile service to try and keep the business alive. This came with setbacks as many clients enjoyed coming to the salon rather than home visits, so some found alternative salons. Still as my appetite for learning had developed I decided now would be the right time to do more, so I set off to train as a teacher.

I was accepted on a teaching course and attended college on a weekly basis, giving me time to run my mobile business whilst I studied. The teaching course took two years, and alongside this I carried out an Assessor's course. Eventually, when my husband and I found a more permanent place to live, I set aside a room in the house to offer treatments, which worked well.

Things still weren't right in my personal life, my relationship was a constant struggle, and I enjoyed the time spent away from my husband working, instead of the time with him. The slightest of things could easily make him turn. It's funny how we think our lives might pan out when the reality can be something entirely different.

Towards the end of my training I took a position at the college as a Beauty Tutor, but had been misinformed about the salary and felt I would be doing far more work than I had anticipated for the salary offered. I decided to sit down with the head of the department to see whether we could come to some middle ground, but she was not offering any sensible resolution. So, as I still had my mobile business to fall back on I gave my notice there and then. To most, this would seem like a drastic move, but for me, it was the brave move I needed.

A short time passed, and I was given the opportunity to train for a degree, that would follow on from the teaching qualification I had gained. I never thought I would have the opportunity to attend University, but it would open more opportunities now, and for the future. It was hard at times, as there was more studying and writing involved than I had anticipated, but I persevered.

My life was changing in so many ways now, and education had helped me along the way to reach goals that I had only dreamt about, especially as I never seemed to enjoy school when growing up. One of my passions that I decided to reignite was my love of exercise and when a new gym opened, I decided to join.

Having been to gyms for years undertaking cardio, weight training, and aerobics exercise, I decided now would be a good time to take a gentler approach. My friend and I would meet weekly for Yoga classes, which was something that I had never done before, but thought it might be interesting. Yoga opened a door to many new possibilities in my life as it made me more flexible than I had ever been, and helped me physically, mentally and spiritually. It opened my mind to bring clarity and inner peace. It was a place where I could relax, away from everything else and leave all my troubles behind; a place where I felt I belonged. It was a part of me, and I could see and feel that Yoga was now going to be my thing and so here I was ready to embrace it with open arms.

I took Yoga classes every week. It was much more than exercise for me; it was about becoming more spiritually aware, allowing energy, good energy at that, to pass through my body. Life seemed quite tough for me at this time, I was still young, and home life never seemed to improve, but I never had the strength to leave either.

There were times when my husband would use emotional threats against me, or threaten to harm the pets. Once he said he'd drown the cats in the fish-tank if I didn't do as he said, or that he would put the cats in the car and take them to the park and deliberately let them go, so that I would not see them again. He even told me that if I didn't get rid of some of my 'stuff' he would get a skip and throw it all in. He even went as far to try and throw me out of the house on the

1st anniversary of my Dad's death, packing my suitcase and throwing it down the stairs.

The emotional threats progressed to physical abuse and the years continued like this. Maybe it made him feel like a strong man against my petite frame, knowing that I would simply have to surrender. My life was not a happy one, and the stress and strain of the relationship often caused me pain not only in my head and heart but more physically in my chest.

Eventually, the pain in my chest got worse, and I decided to visit my doctor and discovered that I was suffering from stress. I tried to ignore this so that I could get on with the parts of my life that I did enjoy, knowing that there was always someone far worse off than myself, and at least now I had Yoga. My interest in Yoga deepened as I started to practice at home as well as attending classes, and I also took up Pilates. The class practices were good in helping to familiarise me with the poses and work in a group and learn from others, but self-practice at home was about developing to a level where I could go much deeper into the practice, and find ways to be my true self.

CHAPTER THREE

Learning, Growing and Serving

Life is About Learning, Growing and Serving

Some of you may spend your lives in search of your destiny, looking for the dream job, dream partner, and the dream family. What happens when you give up searching? Without this focus in your life you don't truly exist. You have been given this life, to serve others and to grow. Some may not understand how they can serve but everyone can, no matter who you are or what you do.

Let's take a school for example. All the staff work, either on a paid or voluntary basis to help others. At each level there are many roles. The school crossing patrol helps children cross the road safely. School governors provide leadership and accountability and make important decisions for the school to run efficiently. Caretakers make sure everything works as it should; including opening the gates in the morning for the children to go to their lessons and closing them again to keep them safe. Dinner Attendants make sure the children are fed at lunchtime and assist with playtime. Secretaries take the calls when children are sick or unable to attend, they make calls to parents, write newsletters and important information leaflets and provide details online to keep parents, teachers, volunteers and governors up to date. The PTA or PTFA, volunteer their time to fundraise for the schools. Teaching Assistants help the teachers and pupils to ensure they benefit from their learning. Teachers provide a comprehensive education to children, teaching them vital lessons they need to grow and develop in life. Head Teachers ensure the school runs smoothly, taking the responsibility to ensure that the teachers and pupils make the right decisions in teaching and learning.

All roles are important, some may seem more important than others, but all are necessary for the effective running of the school. So, no matter what your job role is, don't think that it's not important.

Serving people, animals and nature, is the way for a more harmonious world, where you give your time, ideas, support, and encouragement when required. These acts of kindness can mean a great deal to someone in need, depressed, lonely, struggling financially or who needs advice or support when every other avenue has failed.

There are many ways to help people, without expecting anything in return. For example, in organisations, the travelling costs of those who wish to volunteer could be paid. This would make it easier for potential volunteers to get involved in programmes that encourage engagement with people, develop their confidence and motivate them to go on and repeat this process of helping and serving. Instilling the importance of serving others in need is vital for gaining empathy and compassion for others and strengthening local communities.

The life of serving others is self-generating in the sense that each time you give you receive. Think about it. If you give your time, your ideas and your support freely, how can that help you? Well, it does. You build compassion and develop empathy giving you a greater understanding of what others go through. If you ever face these situations yourself, you will have a better idea of how to cope or adapt. You open yourself up to discover and meet new and interesting people along the way, to make friends and probably lasting ones at that. It helps change mindsets that assume you only do something for a tangible reward, when in fact you don't.

You start to grow in abundance for you soon discover that by giving you also receive and in this case, what you receive is far more than you give. You start to realise that you have more talent, ideas, inspiration and creativeness than you knew. You adopt a more mindful approach and become aware of others and their surroundings so much so that you start to become more generous as you grow. You start to think about all that you can give rather than all that you can take, and with this, the shift occurs. It will come back repeatedly, and once it's gone you may have something new to learn, and the process will repeat itself, but as your mindset changes, you re-focus from helping yourself to helping others.

What Makes You Happy is Worth Holding onto

Never give up something that makes you happy unless it deliberately hurts others. There are many points in this book where I talk about valuing other people's opinions. Becoming more empathetic towards others and helping where you can. Sometimes your behaviour may have been selfish. There may be things you enjoy where you don't consider others or things you enjoy that you know are not good for you.

For example, relationships.

When you start a new relationship the other person may tell you things about themselves, what they enjoy and what they don't. Sharing each other's feelings and interests and getting to know all about the other person helping to build common ground. If you like what you hear, you may want to spend more time with the person as you enjoy their company. Here comes the bit when you decide on how much time you are prepared to give. Do you stop going to the clubs or associations you used to attend? Do you stop your weekly Yoga classes, dance classes, gym workouts, family meet ups, friend's night out? How far are you prepared to go? If it's something you enjoy, don't give it up unless you are happy to do so, as you may later wish you hadn't.

Be as open as you can with the other person about how the things you enjoy make you feel, tell them about the satisfaction they give you. Ask them to join you, that way you get to spend more time together doing the things you enjoy without feeling like you are sacrificing anything. There must also be an element of give and take. Ideally, you should only give up what you knowingly won't hold against the other person or draw attention to later, especially in a heated moment. Another option is to change the day or time that you go if it's an exercise class there are probably other classes on different days and times. I believe everyone must make changes to grow and this includes growing as a couple as well as an individual. It shows a willingness to accept changes which will be vital for the relationship in moving forward and growing.

Never stop smiling because of someone else. Remember no one controls you, so make decisions based on what you know and feel is right. Think of karma in each situation. If you deliberately do something that you know will hurt others, then you will probably hurt yourself in the long run as karma will always return to you, what you give.

So, hold on to what makes you smile, what gives you joy and contentment and with the rest, let it go.

Relationships

Sometimes you may reflect back to past relationships and think, why was I with that person. In the beginning, they seemed fun, charming, and charismatic but hiding beneath the surface was who they were. Think back to how you were at the time. Were you in a balanced state of mind? Were you ready to start a relationship? Were you feeling vulnerable or unloved? Did you feel so low that anyone who gave you companionship, a moment of happiness would seem appealing or did it cause damage?

When you look back, you often see people for who they were. You may have changed intellectually, spiritually or in other ways and are no longer the same as before. Your mind and body may respond on a different energy level than before, and you no longer find this type of person appealing.

Sometimes you will send out energies to others, which connect to your vibrations. When you become in tune with your higher frequencies, you can use this as a guide to attract the good and repel the bad from your lives. *"A true relationship is having someone who accepts your past, supports your present, loves you and encourages your future"* - Unknown

Parenthood

Your parent's or guardian's role is one that should be loving and nurturing towards you from child to adulthood, and hopefully, this was your experience. They are normally the first people that you love and who love you. They are there to help you in your development from the day you were born. They should do this by protecting you, seeing to your needs, supporting you and showing encouragement along the way. They are your first ever teacher helping you to gain your independence, they are there to help you take your first steps, speak your first words, show you how to feed independently and to help you write your first letters and words. But as you become more aware of your surroundings, you soon start to realise that not everyone's life is like this.

Not everyone has the closeness or bond that others have with their parents. Some don't know who one or both parents are. Some are adopted, others are pushed to one side, and some are left not knowing where they belong.

Many parents will divorce, and the family situation becomes messy, with children being used as a bargaining tool, where one or both parents want to cause the other as much pain and suffering as possible in a bitter dispute. Children are used as ammunition in their parent's war. These divorcing parents allow their minds to become bitter and twisted as they seek revenge, which in this way, is the same as choosing dark over light.

My childhood was not straight forward but was still a loving one, in fact, I was never starved of love and affection.

I was born to my mother and father out of wedlock in the late seventies, at a time when a lot of mothers in a similar position were told to give up their children. To top it off they were of different ethnic backgrounds, one being white British and the other Indian, which made it seem even more unusual, especially in the part of Britain that I was born. Where I lived, most people were white. Both my parents had a passion and need to be together until the inevitable happened when they discovered they were about to have a baby. I was created through the yearning for togetherness by two young adults not prepared to be parents nor start a life together, who were enjoying each other's company, until their moments of fun, developed into a serious responsibility, one that they had not planned for—another life.

Neither of my parents was of a mature age or mind. My mother was still living at home at nineteen, and now she was about to experience her first real responsibility. In the months to follow, I continued to grow inside her womb, to a woman who was still young for her years and not ready for this commitment. My maternal grandmother talked the situation over with my mother and offered her a choice, the same one my biological father had offered her, an abortion. Although abortions were a bit taboo then. They thought that would be the best option for her in going forward with her own life. The burden to carry me for nine months would be lifted from her body, freeing her from a commitment to parenthood. With my father offering to pay, the decision could be very straightforward. After some careful consideration of this option, she decided to turn it down.

My mother and father separated, as would most couples who were not ready for a commitment like this and disagreed on whether I should or shouldn't be born. My father came to see my mother when I was about two months old; I guess he thought that now I was born he should ask her to get married. This came with conditions; he wanted to change my name to an Indian one and he wanted me to take his surname. My mother decided against this, and they never spoke to each other again.

I was born a healthy baby and was surrounded by love and warmth from my family. I lived with my mother at my maternal grandparents' house, where they both resided along with two of my mother's sisters. The house was always busy with the six of us. It was a happy upbringing, even though I never met my biological father after this visit.

When I was five, I went to my grandfather and said, "Granddad, I don't want to call you grandad anymore, I want to call you Dad from now on," and that's exactly what I did. It was not something that was expected of me, but it felt right and besides everyone else in the house called him Dad, so why should I call him anything different. I was very fortunate to have him in my life, as I could not have asked for a better father than him.

My biological father, now out of the picture, had two brothers who ironically married two of my mother's other sisters. My mother had five sisters in total all born to the same parents; they ranged from teenagers to adults at the time, except for one that died at the age of eleven, before I was born. She had unfortunately suffered for many years with an illness causing kidney disease. Her illness occurred in the late sixties when regrettably the health service did not have the capability that it has today.

My two aunts who married my biological father's brothers did so out of love, and for a long time seemed happy, all living together in one house in the big city. This was until my paternal grandmother lost her husband. My grandmother was an Indian woman now living alone in Tanzania, who decided to come to live with her sons in England. Her presence and habits were a cultural shock to my aunts, as she behaved in ways which were different from the customs that they were used to in England. My grandmother saw the wives and children as inferior to her as she took on the position of the matriarch, rather than the self-invited guest. She would enjoy mealtimes eating together at the kitchen table with her sons whilst the wives and children would eat together in the hall. When disposable nappies were easily available, they were not allowed to use these and instead had to make their nappies from cloth and sew all the bits together for their babies. With no washing machine, nor any space for one, they would have to hand wash these out in the garden, scrubbing them until they were clean to wear again and hang them out to dry.

About twice a year my aunts and uncles would visit and have short weekend stays with us, and sometimes bring along my paternal grandmother. At the time, as a pre-schooler, I was unaware of who she was. On one of her visits, still unaware of her being my paternal grandmother, I said to her. "Where does my Dad live?" He also lived in the same house as her, but I did not know this. I cannot recall her response, or why I asked her instead of anyone else, but it was a feeling that she was the one with the answers. I think this was the start of me becoming aware of something else inside that could help me. For here I was, not alone but being guided by what many years later became known to me as my guardian angel.

Life went on, and I was growing up fast as children always seem to. I felt somewhat different to everyone else at the time, my complexion was much darker than others at home, and I even started to wonder if I was adopted. My Mum assured me I was not and explained that my Dad was not white, hence why my skin was dark. It seemed to reassure me at the time. I never asked that many questions about my real father as the family didn't seem to like him or want to discuss anything about him and I never even had a photo to see what he looked like.

At the age of five, we decided to get a pet and Dad (grandad) wanted a dog, now that he had retired from coal mining. He kept himself busy and was a DIY enthusiast, always building things such as an ornamental well, bird's houses and dog kennels. But he wanted to get more exercise and having a dog seemed like a perfect solution as well as offering protection for the house. Dad chose a large German shepherd. He couldn't see himself with something smaller. I was fortunate enough to help choose the puppy, and he was cute. In the beginning, I used to pick him up in my arms, but anyone that knows how big Alsatians become will understand that this wouldn't be for long, as he soon became too heavy and too big for me to carry.

He wasn't our only pet though we had a whole menagerie of pets at home including a feral cat that came from a farm. I once pulled his tail and soon got a scratching that taught me not to do that again. We had tons of gerbils, so many in fact that we had to keep them in the greenhouse in the garden, as they were breeding so fast, we had to try and split them up. That was until the feral cat managed to find its way inside the greenhouse one day and killed them. The cat's killer instinct was still present, and is with most cats, whether they are domesticated or not. Like many other cats, it had no interest in eating the prey, but performed a cat and mouse game without understanding the difference between play and kill until there was nothing left to play with.

Then came Cuddles my beautiful black and white cat. He had white paws and three furry white heart shapes covering his neck, chest, and stomach. He was a lucky cat that I should have called him that, as it was by chance that he was saved from death, but I had already used this name for my pet goldfish, won at a local funfair, which I am glad to say is a prize that has been banned in England now. The closest thing you can now win to a goldfish in a bag of water, is a bottle of water.

One day whilst I was at infant school my Mum and Nan took a walk into town, which was not far from where we lived at the time. During their walk, they heard cat noises coming from a box that a man was carrying. They proceeded to ask what was inside, and the man replied, "Two kittens, a male, and female, you can have them if you want. Otherwise I am taking them to the Vet to be put down." Back then people didn't seem treat animals in quite the same way, as we do now. There weren't as many rehoming centres for a start, and people were not that appreciative of neutering their pets (hence the number of Gerbils we had). My mother decided to save one of the cats and took a male kitten and brought him home. They decided against the female, as they thought she would soon have her own set of kittens, and that would be too many to deal with.

After school that day my mother came to walk me home, and as we crossed the road heading towards the local convenience store. I said to her "We have a cat don't we." I had been at school all day and had no hint from her to make this assumption, so theoretically, I had no way of knowing this. She carried on walking, not saying anything and we continued to the shop, and sure enough, she bought a small tin of cat food. I think my Mum thought what I had said was a lucky guess, but I knew it wasn't, because I felt it. It was like something or someone inside me; a little voice told me that we had a cat. It felt like an energy connection possibly with my angel or a telepathic thought from my mother without either of us realising it (maybe you too have had an experience like that, a one of knowing). Anyway, I was allowed to choose my kittens' name, and all I could think about was hugging him. He was so adorable, so I called him Cuddles, and from that day on that was what he was called.

Growing Up

When I was younger, I thought about how one day I would be a parent and all the exciting things I would do when I was a mother; now I wasn't sure when I'd be ready to be one. After six years of marriage, the days seemed to blend into each other, working and studying.

One day as I did the housework I stumbled across an envelope on the floor by my husband's side of the bed, it was opened and bore a hospital stamp. Thoughts immediately filled my head that he was seriously unwell and needed medical treatment, yet he hadn't mentioned anything to me. I picked it up and slowly opened it. I stood there quite shocked with what I had found—we both hoped one day we would probably have kids, now this letter suggested otherwise.

As I read through, I found out that there was nothing medically wrong with him, but that he had arranged to have a vasectomy. How could he make this decision without consulting me? This relationship was based entirely on what he wanted. I wasn't sure how to bring this up but felt I had to. I could feel my blood boiling with the shock and anger, and now I had to confront him when he came home. He initially shouted at me for reading the letter. When he calmed down, he blamed me for not having a child yet. I felt I shouldn't be persuaded by anything I wasn't ready for. I asked him how the doctor had decided without consulting me on what I thought about his vasectomy. He told the doctor that we both decided we didn't want kids, and as he had a child years ago, the doctor agreed. I emphasised that because I didn't have kids yet, it doesn't mean I didn't want them at all. I wanted them later—only not yet. His response was we should either have them now or not at all.

It took me a while to absorb this, and I wanted a couple of days to think it over. I felt perhaps I was wrong for not having kids yet. After all, he was fourteen years older, and I needed to take on board that he didn't want to spend his life looking after kids, but I didn't want the option taken away from me, so as his wife, I agreed that we would try. After nearly five months I fell pregnant. The moment I found out wasn't how I expected it to be; it wasn't a moment of joy and excitement. It was the mere realisation that I was pregnant and not feeling ready, not appreciating it and doubting whether I should have gone ahead with it. But if I was going to stay with my husband I had to agree to it. Otherwise the chance to have children would be taken away.

Over the weeks I started to get used to the idea, the midwife came and checked everything was fine, and a few weeks later I was due for my three-month scan. As the scan drew closer, I started to think of a name, although in my head the baby's name had already been decided. My husband and I were Star Trek fans, and one of my favourite characters was Deanna Troi. We decided that if it was a girl, we would call her Deanna and if it was a boy, we would call him Troy. Deanna seemed right to me, as I had a connection with my nan Annie or Anna as the name used to come into my head, and I wanted to include her name, even though I had never met her, and to me, it wasn't too far off from Deanna. Troy also related to the historical character Helen of Troy who was a strong and bold woman. After the first scan I felt more connected to the baby, and even though we were not told the gender, I had a strong feeling it would be a girl.

My husband purchased a laptop to replace our old computer and desk. I promised the computer and desk to my cousins and agreed to drop them off and asked my husband to help me to take them to the car. When we opened the boot, he couldn't get them in, so I suggested rotating the desk, but he started to shout, insisting it was not going to fit. I said it would, and that we needed to turn it around. He told me to do it if I thought I could and then he pushed me hard against the car and walked off leaving me to deal with it. I was hurting a lot but tried to lift the desk myself despite my discomfort and the weight of the desk. At the time I was a fitness fanatic, exercising a lot and was going daily to the gym so felt strong enough, and with some perseverance, I eventually managed to lift it into the car

As usual, I received no apology from him and over the years I had got into a mindset of accepting his behaviour towards me and how I should be treated—I pretended that nothing had happened and went straight to bed. The next morning, I discovered I had bled in the night. I said nothing to my husband, and after he left, I took the computer and desk in the car to my cousins. I phoned my Mum as I had told her I was pregnant, but I was not ready to tell anyone else yet since I was getting used to the idea myself. The bleeding continued and didn't seem to be slowing. My Mum suggested I took a pregnancy test, so I bought one before heading to the local 'ladies' to carry out the test and waited for the results. I stood there with the kit in my hands waiting patiently for the results—it still showed I was pregnant. I was relieved, but it did not feel right, and I told my Mum this. I bought another test to repeat it later that day, which again showed I was pregnant.

I phoned the hospital to say I was bleeding heavily and that I had taken a pregnancy test that still showed a positive result. I was already due for a scan the next week. I asked the nurse if she knew whether this meant that I had suffered a miscarriage. She indicated that it was hard to say without the scan, which they tried to move forward, but they were fully booked. So now I had to wait. To make matters worse, I heard that an old friend had died, which came as a shock.

I waited patiently for the day of my scan. My husband was aware of what was happening, and he came with me for my scan. The scan showed that I had lost the baby. I thought I had but could not understand why the pregnancy test showed I was pregnant. The test I used showed even low levels of the HCG hormone and whilst this normally happens, it was not useful for my situation.

The hospital said I could come in to remove the foetus or wait to see if it would be removed naturally. I opted for the later. Eventually, the stomach cramps caused me to go back to the hospital to check if the miscarriage was fully completed. It was not so I had to go to the hospital to have the foetus removed. I dreaded the thought of going in, it already felt like every time I used the toilet parts of the foetus would come away from me, and I would start to think about each bit as a part of the baby; its hands, its feet, and body. I felt it was partly my fault for not wanting the baby in the beginning when the pregnancy had taken me by surprise.

I was told I would not be allowed to drive home after the hospital procedure and that I should have 24-hour care. The day was booked, and I had hoped my husband would come with me, but he declined, stating he needed to pick his staff up and wouldn't have time. I felt hurt, we had lost our baby, I was going into hospital to have the foetus removed and he couldn't be bothered to take me but was happy to make an effort to pick his mate up for work. I phoned Mum who told me she was going away and so could not come to the hospital either. No one else knew that I was pregnant, so I couldn't ask anyone else. As I knew I wasn't going to be able to drive back, I decided to walk the three-mile journey to the hospital. I eventually got there crying inside, feeling hurt, sad and alone.

I needed to sit down and rest for a while. I didn't know what to do. I asked my Dad, who had died, for guidance, to show me a sign to make me happy again. I looked out the window and saw the car park and a grassy patch. There was one person sitting next to me, and opposite was another person and a row of empty chairs. I sat there looking around the almost empty room and looked at the empty chairs, and underneath one chair I saw my sign.

Signs come in many forms. Some people see feathers, coins, numbers that repeat themselves. Some hear voices; some are drawn to certain writings or music—when you are open to a sign and pay attention, it comes.

Directly opposite me, underneath the chair was a fifty-pound note. I smiled to myself and knew it didn't belong to any of the people waiting but had no idea how I was going to pick it up discretely without anyone noticing. My heart started to pound. What if someone else came in and picked it up? What if I was called in? I had to find a way to the money up before anyone else saw it.

The chair had a pile of magazines on it. I decided my best option was to head over to the chair, take a magazine and quickly bend down and pick it up. I felt euphoric; it was the perfect sign, a distraction to help me forget about the pain I was suffering, it put a smile on my face when smiles were the last thing I was feeling capable of, and now I had extra money to spend or to save for something nice. I felt slightly guilty when I picked it up, but I knew I wouldn't ever know who it had belonged to or how it got there, only that it had appeared after the moment I had asked for help and had it been someone's purse or wallet I would have handed it in without hesitation, so I sat back down, before it was my turn to be called.

My time came, and the anaesthetist prepared me. Afterward, when they woke me, I went into shock, I was shaking so much I was given extra blankets to raise my body temperature back to normal. I drifted in and out of sleep, feeling weak and tired. Finally, they rang my husband as he had not called to say he was coming for me. An hour later he came, as always, his work came first. I didn't cope very well with waking up, and I was quite sore internally but knew it had to be done; it was a slow walk back to his van. A wheelchair would have helped a lot.

He took me home and asked what I needed, and for a while he was attentive, but soon he got fed up tending to me, whilst I lay in bed trying to rest. I asked for a drink to which his response wasn't very nice. I asked him if he was working in the afternoon the next day. He replied that he was working early in the morning. I told him he was supposed to be looking after me for 24 hours, to which he became angry and turned off the television. He took the remote control, lifted the lower end of the mattress and put it underneath, knowing I wouldn't be able to retrieve it in my condition. He then went out leaving me alone. I lay there and cried. I knew the tears would do no good. I felt totally alone; there was no one there to hear me or support me through this.

After a while he came back to check on me, I was still in bed at this point, so he went back downstairs and watched TV until nightfall. He got into bed that night, fell asleep and left early in the morning, leaving me without help.

Sometimes one of the hardest things to deal with when you are in a relationship like this is, not the consequences of someone's actions, but the feeling of being alone and having no one to support or care for you. Even though I knew my family did care about me, I had kept my early pregnancy private, as many women do, to surprise them once I had been given the all clear, now things had gone wrong, there was no one to talk to.

A few days later my indoor pet rabbit was scratching at her cage. I went to see what was wrong. I went over to pick her up and noticed that there were maggots around her bottom. I assumed she must have a cut where flies had laid its eggs. I tried to wash her to clean away the maggots, then I thoroughly dried and feed her. She seemed a lot better, but the next day the maggots reappeared. Again, I cleaned her, then I took her to the Vet. They looked her over and gave her an injection to stop the infection and said that it was fly strike which is common with rabbits.

It occurs when the animal cuts itself and a fly lays eggs in the wound. The eggs hatch and the larvae feed on the rabbit's wound, eating its flesh. There was therefore a strong possibility that there were maggots inside her too. The Vet offered to keep her in and clean her although they could not see any larvae. I chose to take her home, as what they had described to me did not sound good at all. I had her on my lap for a while at home, stroking her then eventually I put her back in her cage. She soon let out a huge yelp and died.

Within three weeks, a friend had died, my baby had died, and now Tara my rabbit too. I had learnt to control my emotions over time, so that I cried alone and not in front of others. It was hard at first, but I often got told off for crying by my husband, that I soon stopped altogether.

My brother-in-law came to visit and asked what was happening. It was very hard talking to him, I tried to blame my reasons for being upset on my rabbit's death, but I couldn't talk properly, as it was an accumulation of all the deaths I had experienced.

As the weeks passed, I was back at work and tidying the house again. Upstairs in the bedroom I found another letter from the hospital, addressed to my husband, it had already been opened. I read it to discover again about a vasectomy. At first, I thought it must be the same letter I had previously read but, when I checked the dates it was another appointment. Unbelievably, my husband had gone behind my back again to do this. He had told his mates about it too—that now I had lost a child I didn't want another one. I certainly didn't want one straight away after the experience I had. The nurses advised me to wait at least five to six months so that I could come to terms with what had happened. He did not want to wait, as some friends of his had undertaken vasectomies, so he thought he would too. I was again under pressure from him to decide to have a child now for him to put off having a vasectomy. So, we tried again. This time I was going to make sure I was more careful, with the amount of exercise I did on the run-up to the pregnancy, and tip-toe around him, to try and prevent losing this child.

I later went on to have two children a boy named Troy and a girl named Deanna. I wasn't sure whether to use the names still, but it felt right. I felt I knew what I was having both times and was very fortunate to have the beautiful children I have. Soon after my daughter was born, my husband had a vasectomy, but this time I didn't intervene.

My world changed through being a mother. Things that I once put up with I would now no longer tolerate. Before my daughter's 1st birthday my husband and I quarrelled, as we often did. He decided to lock my son in his van and refused to let him out. That for me was enough. It was one thing to tolerate his unacceptable behaviour towards me, but I found it intolerable to allow his behaviour to affect my kids. This was the end of our relationship and the start of something new for me.

I moved on, and over time I went into another relationship. I was seeing a guy for a couple of years, and things seemed fine for a while, but his jealous behaviour started to take over. He accused me of all sorts of things but mainly of having affairs. He always drank in the evenings and gradually drank more. He no longer wanted us to spend time together after work, instead he spent the time, working on his laptop or falling asleep on the sofa. Life became miserable for both of us, and this affected his behaviour and temper, which became more erratic over time. Once, after returning home from a friend's wedding, he became annoyed about something so took a pair of scissors to his brand-new trousers and cut them up. Another day, he started yelling about something stupid, and wouldn't stop, so I threw a glass of water over him to cool him off, which annoyed him even further. His response was to then accuse me of trying to hit him with the glass, to make me feel guilty. He then retaliated by throwing a sack at me, that I had filled earlier with items for charity. I was by then, screaming and crying. He stormed upstairs to the bedroom smashing the television to pieces with a hammer.

I started to understand how toxic this relationship had become and that I did not want this man around my kids and I. Although, I knew I was deeply in love with him and parting would equally hurt, it had to be done. I had always struggled with toxic relationships, meeting men in vulnerable moments when I was unhappy, or not long having come out of a previous relationship. If I felt happy maybe I would be more selective in whom I chose. We tried to talk it through, but he made many excuses to try and avoid talking and eventually packed his things into sacks, probably to get a reaction from me to sweep everything under the carpet. His bags remained piled up in my living room for two weeks as we tried to carry on as normal, to see how things went but it was not working. I had that feeling again that things weren't ever going to be right, and no matter how much trying we did it was not going to solve this situation.

We had a holiday booked for the following week. I had arrangements in place for the children, but he now decided he did not want to go. I gave him a choice, for us to go away or for him to leave, as I could no longer put up with this feeling of being in limbo. He said he wasn't sure what to do, so I made the decision and told him to leave.

He finally took his belongings and went, with a promise that we would talk and see where it would get us. But for me, the talking should have already been done. I was emotionally hurt that it had come to this and felt I had wasted my time on this relationship. I had done the brave thing and said goodbye.

My next brave moment was to go on holiday alone. I decided to book a different holiday, one nearer to me in

Europe. I phoned a travel agent and booked a full board holiday to Spain for the very next day. No point in waiting around, I thought, because if he phoned, I might change my mind and I did not want to be weak now that I was trying to be strong. I had never been abroad by myself before, and I was a nervous flyer, but something sparked me to go. You need to face your fears, for courage to grow.

I did not want to speak to him when he phoned, but, he kept ringing. He left me a message to say he knew I was abroad as he got an international dialling code when he tried to call me. He told me he was going back to his ex-girlfriend, and he would end his life unless I spoke to him. He said he'd drunk too much alcohol and was going to drive at speed until he crashed. In fact, he made sure he was still getting to me, upsetting and controlling my emotions and in some ways still controlling me. When I chose to speak to him he mostly swore and accused me of sleeping with the staff on holiday; the accusations were not stopping. He also said he wanted us to sort this out when I got back.

My holiday was spoilt. He did not want to go on holiday, but he also did not want me to have one either. The week passed, and I tried to relax given the circumstances, but I was an emotional wreck. I agreed to meet when I got back in England, so I drove over two hours from the airport to see him. When I got to him, he changed his mind and told his friend to say he wasn't there.

He was very different now that I was home and ignored my calls. When we finally met, he was very offish, and on one occasion after this, he told me to go and kill myself. I soon found out that he was seeing someone, which he continued to deny it, but I felt was true.

I didn't want to continue allowing him to hurt me by holding on to something that was going nowhere, while he continued with his manipulative 'dog in the manger' type behaviour, but even when you feel strong, moments of doubt can cross your mind. So, on the journey to work one day, I said aloud to my angels that if I got back with him and it was not right, they should send me a sign. Then a very relevant song came on the radio, I changed the channel, and when I thought of him again, the same song played. I thought it was coincidental at first, that it was a popular song in the charts, but I thanked my angels, and as I did this, a tingling sensation ran down the side of my neck and left arm as if to say we are here for you Donella, when you need us we will always be here.

I texted him and said I knew he was seeing someone else, which he denied again, he then asked to speak to me. I pulled over and took the call, and he admitted that he was seeing someone whom he had met, which seemed like another lie, and proved to me that my angel's guidance was right.

Time went on, and over the weeks, and months he would not leave me alone. He now accused me of being an alcoholic. I am not. I had posted a photo on social media of some friends and I on a night out, he saw this and became jealous. He kept sending songs he wanted me to listen to—so that I would understand what he wanted to say. One was by Johnny Cash called; "Hurt," and he asked if I would take him back. He could not tell me how he had changed, although he said he had, yet he wanted me to promise I would not cheat on him in revenge. He claimed his new girlfriend suggested we should get back together, as if I was an easy commodity to pick up or put down as he chose. I was the one to make that decision, and I didn't want it. I had my self-worth, and I was worth more than that. There were many moments after this that still hurt; no one said you can be strong all the time. But neither was I now going to be weak. I was not the liar, cheat, manipulator, and bully; I was now free again from another toxic relationship.

Life Isn't Plain Sailing

Life isn't plain sailing,
Unless you have a good boat.
But even with a good boat,
There will always be the occasional storms.
Enjoy all the beauty the world has to offer,
Let these experiences inspire you in all you do,
And create fantastic memories along the way.

—Donella Hoyle, January 2017

CHAPTER FOUR

Gratitude

Wanting More

What happens when you don't have what you want? Some of you will be thankful, and content with what you have regardless. You may not be ecstatic about the situation you are in or about the things you have, but you make do, you recognise that life is ever changing and evolving. Things come and go in your lives, and you may still get what you want although it may not be what you expected—those that are content will accept it gratefully, others will be ungrateful and disappointed. Ladan Shaygan wrote this very valid statement, *"Remember that sometimes not getting what you want is a wonderful stroke of luck." Shaygan, L. (Shaygan, 2017).* How true that statement is.

Let's take a child who watches a series of toy adverts on TV and then out shopping sees the same toys for sale. The images of these toys are constantly in its mind. Leading up to Christmas, the adverts are repeated only now they are more intense as they start to play with the child's mind. Then the child asks their parent or guardian for the toy—in my case, it would be, "Mum I want that toy for Christmas, Mum can I have that, Mum I really want it."

The child writes a list of things it wants for Christmas, never including a list of what they will give, such as helping Mum make cakes or biscuits for Christmas. The list doesn't include giving money to children in deprived countries to pay for food. Some may say these are extremes, and that children don't understand these things, but why not?

Schools should teach more about compassion, about understanding the quality and quantity of food available in the world, and how in developed countries food is available on demand from local supermarkets or by having it delivered to your door, cooked and ready to eat. I would add that these lessons should start at home, and be enriched at school.

Do you take the time to speak to your children about the number of miles a day many children in deprived countries who are probably of the same age, have to walk to school—alone as their parents or guardians are without cars? Do you explain to your children that some of these children are unable to go to school because there is no school to go to or no one to pay for their schooling? Do you tell your children how much they already have in comparison to other children around the world? Most of you do not.

Most people in the western world will be thinking about what more you can buy your children, listening to what else they want. This is fuelled by an expectation of the child to get more and more, which is constantly being fed by media adverts that your children watch.

Other parents start to compete. It's a battle of who buys the biggest, newest and most expensive. It may put a dent in your possibly overstretched pockets, creating months or even years of debt for things that might not even be appreciated. You have become conditioned by society to believe that this is a positive thing to do.

The good news is that you can change. That's right you heard it. You don't have to believe this or do this anymore.

The right thing to do is think about what your child needs. For example, do they need a new bike because theirs has got old and rusty or is now too small? Have they outgrown their toys and developed beyond the learning capacities for the toys they have?

Why not restructure how you do Christmas this year? Buy your children toys, but not so many. Buy something you know they will play with and learn from, so it has dual benefits. Discuss with your children that as a family, you will donate some money to children who have no food. In your heart, you know that by giving, you are also receiving. Put some money in your children's bank for a rainy day, or towards your children's future for when they need it, such as a deposit on a car that they may need to get to college, university or work or towards their first house. Whatever it is you decide to do, think before you act. The learning here is to change the mindset and behaviour, from an expectation of wanting and giving more than you can afford, to being grateful for what you and your children have.

Going back to the start of this chapter, what you think your child wants may not be the case. If you always give in to pressure from the consumer culture and your children's demands to have more, they may not enjoy them for very long and even want the next version. How often have you bought something, for it not to be used to its full capacity or for it to be left unopened in the toy box? How many times have your children been disappointed with something you bought them? It may have taken you months to save for it, months to find it, and months of hearing that your child wanted it. Then it all ends in a massive disappointment all around, for your children and for you.

Not having everything you want allows you to be thankful for what you do have. It makes you work towards the things you really need more purposefully. If you dream big and work towards getting what you truly want, you appreciate it so much more.

Why do you think the values of compassion, selflessness, understanding, appreciation, empathy and gratitude are important? I believe everyone should naturally have compassion and be willing to help others, without expecting anything in return. You should acknowledge other people's opinions and feelings even if you don't always agree with them. You should understand how other people's lives are, when different to your own. You should understand how it is to have things you want and how it is to be without those things so that you can empathise with others in a similar situation. You should be grateful for what you have and the opportunities that life affords you.

As a modern society, we have become very wasteful. So many people throw things away that they no longer use instead of recycling, upcycling or donating to others in need. When you live by these values, you have a greater sense of the purpose of who you are. You are more confident and self-assured and better able to maintain focus in your life.

When you teach your children these values, they learn to respect their elders, who share their knowledge and wisdom with them. You give them a firm foundation to start their lives, to shape their future, and become individuals who in turn understand the importance of these positive values and apply them in their lives. You help to develop their life skills so they can become self-sufficient. You support them to build and shape their characters into responsible, caring and kind individuals, who see the world as it should be, not merely as it is. Your children will be more willing and prepared to work for inner peace, world peace and unity.

When you fail to teach your children these values, they are deprived of the wisdom and experience of stepping back and seeing the bigger picture. They are likely to develop the negative traits and behaviours that can come from their unguided development. They may become selfish, always putting themselves before others; haughty, not seeing others as their equals; bitter and resentful, when they fail to get what they want, when they want it, and unable to comprehend what life is like for others. You can change this. It's never too late. Small steps lead to giant leaps.

Second Chances

What happens when things go wrong in your life? Many of you have been there when things don't go the way you expect. This could be through choices you made or the things that happened around you. If your individual choice put you where you are, don't be too hard on yourself if things don't turn out the way you had hoped. If someone did something wrong, especially if that person is close to you, you are likely to forgive them. So why can't you forgive yourself in the same way that you forgive others?

You expect people to treat you with respect and dignity and you know you should treat others in a way they want to be treated, so why punish yourself for a mistake? Mistakes are there so you learn and grow from them; they are not there to make your lives continuously difficult, even though, at the time, it may seem that way. Be kind to yourself, look after yourself, forgive yourself, give yourself another chance to change and make good what you did wrong. Learn from this experience so that it isn't repeated, and if it is, go forward and know how to correct it next time. Be realistic, for everyone makes mistakes in life, and you deserve a second chance, so give yourself all the second chances you need.

A Kiss Can Make All the Difference

Everyone has been there; in a moment, a time or place where things haven't gone smoothly. Then bit by bit the situation gets worse, leading to frustration, annoyance, paranoia, arguments and a dislike for the other person, even if this is a person you are close to begins to grow. There are always different ways to calm a heated moment down; you can walk away or talk to the person about the problems; avoid an argument where you can or take a moment to pause. But have you ever tried a hug or a kiss? (Obviously this is only, if it is someone close to you, not to be tried on the local shop assistant)

A kiss or a hug can make all the difference. Touching someone intimately can bring you back together. It can de-stress you, boost your immune system and can make you realise all that you both have said and done is trivial in the grander scheme of how important you are and how much you mean to each other. By defusing the situation in this way, it shows affection; it shows you care; it shows you love each other—and can make all the difference. If you want to try something similar with the shopkeeper, it is better in these moments to say, 'I'm sorry'; it could save embarrassment or a slap in the face.

The next day, jot down all the things that bothered you so that you don't leave anything out that may start to niggle you. Find time to talk to your partner and go through the things one by one. You may not get a solution straight away that completely settles the situation, but life comes with compromises, so working things through will help defuse things. Sometimes the situation can blow out of proportion if you have an off day; everyone has them. Your hormones might be racing, you may have a headache, or you might be tired or not sleeping well. Remember if you are not feeling one hundred percent you may not act or react in your normal way. However, now that there's less edginess between you both, things should seem a lot easier to deal with.

Barriers

Putting up a barrier doesn't always protect you and it can also hurt you. Let's take relationships. What happens when you meet someone new after being hurt? When you start to have deeper feelings, do you fall in love with them like you have never loved before? Are you open to new experiences and the new love that you are about to experience? Are you still focused on the hurt or suffering from before, so much so that you guard your heart and try and protect your soul? You may choose to put up a barrier so high that you don't let the next person into your life as you should. You think you are protecting yourself, but on the contrary, you harm yourself by not allowing yourself to love and be loved like you should. You think that the higher the wall, the better protected you are in case something goes wrong, in case the person does not turn out as you had hoped, in case the relationship goes stale. In case, in case…

You cannot go on with your life waiting around, causing unnecessary suffering on what may or may not happen. If you are not fully ready to open your heart to accept the love you deserve, then are you ready for a relationship at all? Are you ready to move forward with your life or are you so stuck in that moment of shutting down the love in your heart that it would need a hammer and chisel to chip away at it? You need to face the problem. If it's something from the past, be aware you are not in the past but the here and now, and this is the only moment that exists. This is a new relationship, new time frame, and a new partner, don't bring your old thoughts and feelings into it now. Be open to the possibilities of what this new relationship can bring—prosperity, freshness, newness and other wonderful experiences. Focus on opening your heart chakra, visualising a green colour filling your heart and sternum. Remember don't judge your new love against your ex-partner, or past.

Learning to Say No

My life hasn't always been bad, nor has it been all good, but life is like that, full of ups and downs, highs and lows, and ins and outs.

I've made mistakes in life, hasn't everyone? I have had to reach deep inside, to put things right so that some good could come from the wrong I did. On the contrary, though, had my life been straightforward and without any mistakes to learn from, I probably would not have written this book.

I Feel Good

I feel good when I do good,
I feel sad when I'm bad.
I feel sad when I do bad,
I feel as I should when I do good.

—Donella Hoyle, February 2017

Your lives are ever changing, even for those that don't like change. Change occurs naturally, through your desires or can be sprung upon you; whichever way it happens change comes and is necessary.

One of the hardest things I have found in life was learning to say no. How many of you have had the same problem? When you feel you don't want to do something or shouldn't do something, you want to say no, but instead you say yes. It's happened to me many times in many situations. When I was younger, mainly in my teens, I went along with what others wanted to do, as I felt I would have been pushed aside by my friends. I quickly grew out of this as I got tired of following others, I didn't want to be the sheep anymore and instead opted to be the shepherd.

Being unable to say no did not stop there. Unfortunately, it continued into adulthood, which sometimes happens when you develop habits, you occasionally fall back into the same old ways. The Universe has many lessons to teach you, and once you learn them you can move forward, but when you slip back into your old ways, the lessons present themselves all over again.

I can recall another work-related experience of being unable to say no; I found myself overworked, with extra work pouring in. Instead of saying, "No, I cannot help at the moment," when I needed to, I found myself saying yes. This predominantly came from being a people pleaser, thinking it would help my business, or put a tick next to my name. The problem with this was I would be working on a half full or empty tank and could not give the time and energy needed to do my best work.

If friends, loved ones and family members asked for my help, such as to make a phone call or research something on their behalf that seemed like a quick activity, it would generally take up more of my time than anticipated. Time, which I have discovered as I get older, gets more and more precious.

Having suffered the consequences of a burnout, feeling stressed and unhappy, I now re-evaluate what I do. Instead of quickly saying yes, I usually say I will think about it. If it's something that I am happy to do but unsure of whether I want to commit to it, I will give the reason why I cannot help on that occasion. If I simply don't want to do it, I say no and sorry. Honesty works best here, as it does in all areas of your life, even in those moments when you think it won't. If I am happy to do what has been asked, then I say, yes. This process lets the person know straight away that I am either able to help or not and ensures that I have not committed to anything that I am not happy to do.

Saying no takes time. Don't think that you now have the magic tools to say no straight away. If you do perfect, but if not don't worry. As with anything, take each day as it comes. When faced with situations like this say yes or no with integrity. Make sure you believe your response and say it with calmness and validity. Be true to your words and stick with them. Bear in mind if you were happy saying yes, you would say it spontaneously.

CHAPTER FIVE

Feel Your Pain and Embrace the Change

When someone close to you dies, the feeling is unbearable. It may feel like it cuts you up inside as no other thing can. It is an emotional and painful time. There are always words that have been left unsaid and the feeling deep inside wishing that these had been spoken. When you sleep, the spirits of these people will sometimes visit you. You will find yourself in a dream, or dream state, no longer needing to say the things that you wish you had. When you are in that state, you realise that those unspoken words and thoughts were never that important and what was important was you being part of their life.

Let the people that are important to you in this life know that you appreciate them. Death doesn't necessarily mean the end. In many ways it's the beginning for you; it's a life without that person and a new journey for the spirit of the person who has passed.

The Memory of A Loved One Never Dies

Have you ever seen someone in the last stages of dying, where you knew they only have a short time left to live? Death is not something that should be contemplated until it's your time to go. When you have a near death experience, or you see someone, as I have, dying in front of you, but wanting to live, your thoughts about dying change.

My grandfather, whom I will continue to refer to as my Dad suffered from lung, liver and bowel cancer late in his life. It was one of the most difficult times in my life, and believe me I have gone through the works, as I am sure many reading this have too. I have Hashimoto's thyroiditis which is a non-contagious auto immune disease, it causes an inflammation of the thyroid gland, and instead of protecting the thyroid its starts to destroy it and this caused my thyroid to stop producing enough hormones. The thyroid gland is a butterfly shape gland positioned in the front of the wind pipe. It is a life-long condition that happened to me soon after my first child was born. This condition is more common in women than men and makes you feel tired, causes bloating, slows down your metabolism causing weight gain, lethargy and brain fog. I have found that taking my daily medication, following a careful diet and having a healthy lifestyle including Yoga and meditation, have helped keep this condition relatively stable. But unlike my controlled disease, my father was dying of terminal cancer.

Dad didn't want to give up. He wanted to enjoy life, spend time with his family, grandkids, and pet dog. He came from a generation where men were the providers, yet here he was struggling to do the simplest of tasks, even peeling carrots was a challenge for him. The weakness he was experiencing in his body was only part of the ongoing symptoms yet to come.

He detested the Chemotherapy treatment and said it felt like a burning sensation running through his body. He had to have part of his liver cut away when the inevitable was always going to happen, this would however, buy him a bit more time. But it was his willingness to keep going for as long as he could that gave us strength, for he was a true fighter to the end. He didn't want to die in the Hospice. He wanted to be at home surrounded by the love of his family, not in a hospital bed being dependent on others.

When the pain got worse, morphine was given in small then higher doses, until no one could understand what he was saying, as he became delusional. It must have been so frustrating to be in a body that no longer serves you, that no longer wants to go on, yet your mind does. Eventually, his body could no longer take food as the white blood cells took over, attacking and weakening his body until it could fight no more. The morphine drip was permanently removed, as was the food drip and then all hope started to fade.

Before Dad went to the Hospice, I used to visit him at my family's home. I would sometimes struggle to go to his bedside to sit and talk with him, for he no longer seemed the strong man I once knew. Facing me, instead was this fragile man, needing the care and attention of his family and nurses on a daily basis. Knowing that this was the last thing he would have wanted, making him feel like he was losing his dignity and pride.

I struggled to hold back the tears, as I saw tears as a weakness; a sign of childishness, not womanhood, a sign that I was surrendering. I should have held him and let my tears flow, but I stored them away the best I could. I thought that what I was doing would be for the best all round. I would try and swallow my tears, almost choking on my salvia. My heart yearned to see this man fit and healthy again, so he could do the things he loved and enjoyed. But instead, he was bound by the bed in which he lay.

When he moved to the Hospice I went to see him several times over the couple of weeks he had left and saw him on the day before he passed. The nurses told me that he was no longer taking food or drink. I knew you can survive a while without food, but without water, he was not going to live much longer. Without morphine in his system, he again started to talk like the father I had always known; he joked the way he always did, smiling, making me happy and proud to have him as my father throughout my twenty-one years of life. He had been there to support me, love me, guide me and teach me right from wrong; to be there for me even when I messed up. I shouldn't have even been there as I was unwell, but the need to be with my Dad took over.

Seeing my Dad in this way was one of the things that had a negative effect on my health as did other events in my life at the time. Looking more like a Geisha girl than myself with chamomile lotion all over my face due to an outbreak of Shingles, I wanted to say my last words to him and more importantly for me, to listen to my Dad's final words, before he passed away the next day.

It is with a sad heart that I thanked my Dad for everything he did for me and others. He was a loving man with a kind heart and soul and helped shape me into the person I am now. I could not have asked for anymore. In memory of Dad, you are an inspiration, and I respect and Love you.

Meditation Six: Full Yoga Breath

Let's think about taking some time to relax. Take some deep breaths in and out.

Every time you inhale in, realise you are breathing in life giving oxygen. Each time you exhale out, release stale unwanted air away from the body.

You live a life where every breath counts. It is your connection to Earth, your life-giving energy. With each breath you take, your realisation that you are here can be understood. Breathing can change with your moods and feelings. When you become anxious, your breathing may become erratic and out of sync. When you are upset, your breathing may become long and deep as you feel it is pulling up from your belly through to your lungs. When you exercise your pulse increases, and so does your breath, when you rest or sleep, your breath slows down to a comfortable rhythm. When you are mindful of your breathing you can feel the inhalations and the exhalations so much more than before.

So, with this I want you to join me in a series of breathing exercises known to many as the full Yoga Breath. Find somewhere quiet and comfortable to lie down. You will then proceed by laying on your backs with your shoulders pushing down into the floor and your eyes gently closed.

With your fingertips either side of your navel. Begin by inhaling from the lower abdomen and slowly expanding through the diaphragm the ribcage, the chest, the lungs, the shoulders, holding onto the breath at the top for a moment, then slowly exhaling through the nose, releasing down through the shoulders, the lungs, the chest, the ribcage, the diaphragm, drawing the navel towards the spine. Repeat this process six times in total, being aware of how the body feels on the inhalation and the exhalation. Feel each inhalation restoring the positive energy within you, and each exhalation removing any unwanted stale air away from you, as this can create blockages, so gently release this and any negativity it may hold.

Feel your body increase in positive energy, bringing with it a sense of peace, calm and prosperity and as you exhale release all thoughts of negativity, thoughts of anger and thoughts of not being good enough bringing restoration, peace, and happiness.

Comfort Zones

In your life there will often be situations and events that put you out of your comfort zone. Things may happen that directly or indirectly make you feel uncomfortable. In moments like this, it can be difficult to remain focused, positive and maintain a balanced state of mind. So, what do you do? Do you give up? Do you give in? Do you stop trying to restart? No, I tell you. You need to fight and stand for what you believe in. No matter what tries to disrupt your psyche, your train of thought or your feelings you will sometimes need to step out of your comfort zone to grow.

Help others in need where you can. There may come a time when you too need help and hope that others will help you. I would like you to read a poem I wrote about an event, which indirectly affected me but directly affected so many others. One that brought people together in a time of need, where nothing else mattered apart from unity.

No Need to Fall

Great people never get where they are without a struggle,
Without a fall,
But here I am, and I stand tall.
I will not venture to the dark, for I will shine a light,
I'm not here to back down; I will fight;
But not with fists, with arms or with hatred,
But with words of kindness,
With words of soul,
To reach to those who have chosen to go,
The wrong way through persuasion, through greed,
through lust, through betrayal,
To help them to realise they are important as we are all.
Life is worth living so live it with care,
Life is loving,
So, find somewhere with which to share;
The happiness,
The sadness,
And all the inbetweens,
For together we can fight hatred and be the best human beings.

—Donella Hoyle, June 2017

Visualisation Exercise Two: Law of Attraction

The manifestation of what you desire can happen but only when you are clear about what it is you want. Be clear about the size, the shape, the colour. Let's take a car as an example. What type of car do you want? What model? What year is the car? See that image in front of you, see yourself in the car. Visualise or meditate on you driving the car, parking the car, feeling the interior, seeing yourself happy in the car.

Think about all the actions you are going to take to help bring this car in your life. Even though you are asking you still need to take up any opportunities or situations where you can. Maybe the action you can take may involve taking on more work if it's available to you. Why not have a look through your belongings at home and see if there is anything you no longer want or need that you can sell so that you can put some money aside. What about buying a lottery ticket and choosing numbers that are relevant to you. Whatever action you can think of, at least try three things.

Once you have put this action forward to the Universe, start to pay attention to signs you see, for they are unlikely to come as a clear message, but as guidance. It may be a name of a street, numbers that keep reappearing, maybe you see the car you want more so than ever, or something completely different, but start to pay attention, as once you start to realise what they are, more will come.

Stay positive with what you want, don't become disheartened if it has not materialised the next day. Anything good that comes into your life needs to be appreciated. Feel good about what you have in your life already. Undertake things that make you feel good like meditating, listening to music, spending time with your friends or family or even relaxing in the bath with some candles.

Do not put barriers in the way of achieving what you

want, don't put negative aspects in place, such as I am not going to get this, I don't deserve this. Don't allow yourself to get frustrated. Instead make positive statements like I will have the car I desire, it's going to look like this and I will be happy in having it, I will not let anything silly get in the way of my desire.

If you have called upon the Universe to manifest what you desire you need to fully support your manifestation as it presents itself to you, so reach out and grab it before it's gone. Depending on what it is you may need, you sometimes have to put yourself before others. It may mean putting your job or career on hold, but don't let this opportunity pass you by otherwise it may go to the next person, whose vibrations are on the right frequency. Are you willing to risk this passing through your hands? If you have called this to you and then let it go, did you want it in the first place? Are you one of those people who are prepared to let the opportunities pass you by? Are you one of those people who wants to look back with regret or one who looks on it with happiness as you took the chance when it presented itself to you? If you let it go, the Universe will probably move its energies towards the next person that is open and willing for this opportunity.

Take a job vacancy for example; if you don't apply, you don't stand a chance of getting the position. However, once you apply, you stand a better chance than if you had not applied. If you attend the interview without putting your energy into it, then someone else will, so think about giving it all you've got, that way if you are not successful at least you know you gave it your best, rather than thinking you should have tried harder.

I will you to succeed in everything you do in life. So, act on your desires, listen to your instincts and stay focused on what you truly desire.

Balancing Work, Life, and Family

Have you ever thought about how things work well in your life when they are balanced? Your work, life, family, health, and leisure are all things that need to be equally balanced for them to have a positive effect on your life. How balanced are these areas in your life? In the section below, I would like you to work through the exercises below with me.

Let's start by taking three of these areas. You can randomly choose three. For this exercise, I will use work, health, and family. Using these or your own choices decide which order they currently feature, in your life? Write down your answers, so that you can refer to these later.

Now looking at the three areas again which order do you think your three choices should be in, to make you feel happy and contented? Don't worry at this stage if you think changing them is not an option; write down your ideal. (Remember positivity here is the key). Looking at your answers, why do you think they are in the sequence they currently feature in?

Are you feeling off balance? If so which ones come first? This is most likely to be the one that is causing you to be off balance and probably is the one that takes up most of your time and attention. So now you know which order you would like them to be in—what is the first in your sequence? Is it the same? If not, this could predominantly be the one whom you would like to give more of your time and attention.

So now thinking again about the order you ideally want. How do you think, you can change this to make it so? Does it seem like a massive task or does it feel like you need to make minor adjustments here? Are these things you can change today? Or do they need a bit more time? Is it time with the family you wish for? Is it more quality time rather than quantity?

Family

Here is what I would like you to do. I want you to find your alarm clock and reset it for 15-20 minutes earlier than normal, then come straight back. If you value your sleep, I want you to go to bed earlier by the same amount of time. So, if you have set your alarm to wake up 15 minutes earlier, then you need to go to bed 15 minutes earlier as well.

Avoid caffeine in food or drinks for at least a couple of hours before bed, as you need your mind to be calm and still and not stimulated.

Next, I want you to set aside 10-20 minutes to meditate. You can use one of the meditations I have included in this book, one of your own or one you have sourced elsewhere, use what works best for you. Once this is done, take yourself off to bed. In the morning you should wake up feeling refreshed, energised and ready to start the day anew.

Now use your morning time wisely. Why not make breakfast for everyone? You could set the table with bowls and cutlery, make some toast, boil some eggs and share the wonderful experiences of eating the most important meal of the day together as a family. If that's not possible during the weekdays, then try it at the weekend or meet up with your family to share lunch, during the week if you can.

Work

Is your work affecting you? What is it about your work? Is it the people with whom you work? Your boss? The type of work you undertake? The hours you currently work? The time it takes to get to work? Your position? The reasons could be one or several of these things or maybe one not even mentioned here, but whatever it is you need to address it so you may rectify it.

Make a list of all the things that have come up from the above questions. See if there is anything within the list you can change to make you feel more balanced.

Maybe you have the type of job where if you put in extra hours, or arrive earlier you can leave earlier and spend more time with your loved ones; whatever it is small changes can and need to be made.

Health

Is it your health that needs to be prioritised? Do you feel some parts of you don't fully function like they used to?

So, one hour before bed, run a warm to hot bath and add some bath soak or even make one for yourself. An example of this would be to put a few drops of essential oil such as Lavender in half a cup of milk under running water to disperse the oil, this way you can also inhale the oil. Then when it is time for your soak, have a body scrub ready to wash all that dry skin from your body, leaving you with fresh, rejuvenated skin. You can even make a scrub of your own, as they are simple to make. I have included one in my later chapters, but here is another to get you started.

Use half a cup of sugar, half a cup of olive oil or coconut oil and a few drops of essential oil and mix all the ingredients together then pop them into an airtight container. That way you have more for another day. Use as little or as much as needed for a full body scrub and once you emerge from the bath and have dried yourself off, moisturise your body and slowly feel your body thank you. Then sit somewhere quiet

*to meditate for 5-10 minutes, if you are used to meditating
you can go longer than this. Work with your body and as
I wrote in the previous section on Family, take yourself to
bed. Lie on freshly cleaned sheets and enjoy your sleep to help
your body to restore its energy and health again. Sleeping is
important for good health. If you are used to going to bed
late, try to go to bed a little earlier, so that you allow your
body time to self-heal and relax.*

Gratitude

As you get older, you tend to lose the sense of what you truly
want and need. When you are a baby, you seek love and
attention. You do this through a series of interactions with
your parents, but as you get older your needs change, and you
become centred on the thoughts of more tangible things that
generally cost money. What grounds you, are the things that
cost nothing, the most important of which is love.

Being grateful for what you have now, has a big impact
on how you feel about life. It helps you focus on the present
moment, the here and now, not imagining what might happen.
Everything you learn can be useful, but you may not see this
immediately. Unless you appreciate what, you have achieved
to date, much of the knowledge may seem irrelevant or a waste
of time, but it is not. You have come far in your journey and
still, have far to go. Your gratitude should be part of your
mindset, and you should be as grateful for the big things as
you are for the small things. Having enough bread to make
toast, enjoying your morning cup of tea or coffee before work,
enjoying a moment of stillness and peace as you sit, are small
things that you may take for granted. Name one thing you
are grateful for today?

When you break it down in this way, you soon see that
there is so much to be grateful for in your daily lives.

Victims

A victim is a powerless person. How often have you been a victim or seen yourself as the victim? You may be a victim of domestic abuse and have been hurt physically and mentally. You may have been bullied, harassed, stalked or even assaulted. You may be a victim of your own abuse, maybe you self-harm or did in the past. Are you a victim of a scam? How often do you hear about people trying to obtain money through dishonesty? Maybe you are a victim of a natural disaster such as a flood, storm, earthquake or tsunami. Do you have an illness and are a victim of it, such as cancer or depression?

Whatever it is causing you to feel the victim, you will continue to be one if you want to stay one. When you decide to get out of this way of thinking and being, you will no longer be a victim. Instead you become the fighter, the warrior, the hero, the survivor. You will realign yourself, restoring balance to your body and mind and bring harmony within. You become the smart person, the intelligent person, the wise person, the person who leads the way to a better future.

So, rise above your negative thoughts of being the victim and change these to positive and releasing thoughts of being the victor. Use your inner strength, to pull you through what you once saw as difficult times in your life. Let the fear and anxiety fade as you let all thoughts of anger or self-blame be gone. This will help you become a stronger person. Let the past be the past. Acknowledge any misgivings and move forward with your life. You survived because you were stronger than you realised. Seek the help you need and offer help where it's useful to others. Speak out, don't let others control you. Instead, lead the way to your new beginnings.

As a society, attitudes towards abuse are changing for the better. What was once left unsaid is now being spoken. The recent Harvey Weinstein sexual harassment scandal that has wrecked the entertainment industry is evidence of this shift.

Laws to protect victims have changed and improved. But they cannot change without your support, without you having the confidence to come forward so that others will too, and the information and support they offer will push forward the laws of change for good.

To turn around a situation where you were a victim or had victimhood forced on you, will take time for healing, to repair and change. Make sure you take the time you need and then find the way to stand tall again. Remember you have nothing to be ashamed of, you have done nothing wrong. You are in a safe place now; nothing needs to hold you back, push yourself forward into the life you deserve, the life you were always meant to have and enjoy.

Louise Hay is such an inspiration to many. She once said, *"Every time you feel like a victim, you're affirming that you want to continue to feel like a victim." (Louise Hay, 2018)* And isn't that so true? How often have you seen yourself as the victim or been the victim? So, rise above this feeling that holds you back, so that people cannot take charge of you or start to feel sorry for your misgivings.

No Longer a Victim

How do you see yourself now? Do you see yourself as some-
one with plans and goals?
Are they in motion or still yet to flow?
Your past is how it should have been, to get you where
you are now.
I have a calling, no longer to be small,
I have this calling to stand tall.
I am all that I am, and more, with my wings, I have
flown,
I was once a child and now look how I have grown.
I am a woman first, a teacher and more,
A speaker, a coach, an author.
I am a therapist and a mother too,
So, see yourself in all that you do.
I am going to dream big for my destiny to occur,
Where my pathway in life is no longer a blur.
I am no longer different, uncomfortable or feeling left out,
I am now this strong, courageous woman, who uses her
voice to shout.
To be vocal, to be heard, to communicate,
I will no longer have to deliberate.
So many experiences, where many were sore,
I'm going to be now, what I adore.
My feelings they hurt,
My voice is unspoken.
My tears I kept,
To stop my heart from being broken.
No longer a mute, I communicate at will,
No longer when I am told,
But when I feel.
So be proud of this strength inside you, as am I,
Be emotional if that's what it takes, you can be a man
and cry.

Let the stigma go and with it all thoughts of
self-conscious,
Awaken your soul to a new preconscious,
And finally, see,
You are now, whoever you want to be.

—Donella Hoyle, August 2017

Misconceptions and Judgements

Have you ever been told something about a person, to find out that in the end it doesn't ring true? Have you either been lied to or been party to a game of Chinese whispers? Have you ever felt that the information passed down to you has been so poorly construed that the reality of what happened or the actual story is something very different indeed?

Do you know something that you have been told about someone to be true, and have then held it against them? How many times have you judged someone on how they looked or how they once behaved? Do you judge people on their past because you judge yourself? As Wayne Dyer once said, *"When you judge another, you do not define them, you define yourself."* *Wayne Dyer 2017.*

Some people learn, grow and expand from their mistakes. Others repeat the same patterns over and over again. *"Humans are wired to master disappointment rather than seek fulfilment."* *Plotner, B. (Plotner, 2017)*

Never give up trying in life. If you do, you are merely existing and not living at all. You were given life from the moment you took your first breath, and all you knew at that moment was the instinct to survive. You needed to breathe to live, you need food to grow, and you needed love to thrive. So why, when obstacles, events, catastrophes, and upsets occur in your life, do you want to throw these amazing experiences away? What if this is your only life, your only chance to make a go of things, to get things right? Are you still willing to throw it all away? What a waste it would be.

Judgements

There have probably been times when you have judged a person on how they have behaved or what they have said but try to look beyond what you think you know about a person and your assumptions may fall apart. Let's do the same here for what you have been told about an animal, an object, insects and more. Don't make judgements on the negative aspects, instead, look only at the positive attributes.

Take a fly for instance. It has the amazing ability to fly at high speeds under difficult weather conditions and vast distances. You all know what they like to gather on and eat. But at least they never judge you by your smell. In fact, if you do smell, they will probably like you even more. The common house fly will never bite or sting you. It will never be your friend, so it will never betray you. It may want to share your meal with you but will leave plenty behind for you, in fact, it would be as happy with your unwanted food. Some flies lay eggs on dead things so that their larvae can eat this, but with so many types of flies, they all have different and specific roles. As far as the ecosystem is concerned they help out in the food chain and are an excellent source of food for spiders, bats, birds, and fish which gather their nutrients and energy from these flies and without them would soon decrease in numbers.

You have probably been previously judgemental and have drawn conclusions, without a solution and believe yourself to be right. But before you next judge, before you next make a bold statement, take a moment to think about the consequences of your decisions. If it leads to you taking action, remember, some mistakes are irreversible.

Take the Dodos, for example; sailors thought it would be a good idea to hunt them as they seemed easy to catch—to a point where their habitats diminished until they existed no more. It's obviously too late now to try and save this extinct bird, and a sad reminder how humans can show disregard towards nature but society needs to have a greater awareness of the consequences of actions taken, as in this case, it destroyed the Dodo's habitat and the Dodo along with it. For other endangered animals, there is still time to try and save them from extinction, such as many birds and insects, including the Bee whose wild habitats are already at risk.

Bees play an important role in the world as they are one of the few insects that pollinate flowers, from which they help pollinate all varieties of fruit, vegetables and more including cocoa, for chocolate. But it does not stop there. Many animals also rely almost exclusively on fruit for food. The diminishing numbers of pollinating bees could be disastrous to the way of life as we know it.

One way to help is to try and encourage bees in gardens by planting flowers they are attracted to such as sunflowers, which are pollen rich. Or even create a wild garden and have areas with small holes in the mortar of the garden walls that masonry bees can use.

Non-Judgemental

Have you heard of a doppelganger? Apparently, everyone has one, maybe even more than one for some. The Cambridge dictionary defines doppelgänger as *a spirit that looks exactly like a living person, or someone who looks exactly like someone else but who is not related to that person. (https://dictionary. cambridge.org/dictionary/english/doppelganger)*

Have you ever looked at someone and thought it was someone you know; only to find out you were mistaken? This has happened to me. I thought I knew someone and every time I saw this woman I thought she was a girl I once knew when I was younger. I remember who I thought she was, who her parents were, her siblings and even how she and I met. We never spoke to each other, and so I didn't know her very well, but still, I thought I remembered her. I started to see her almost every day when she dropped her children off at the same school that one of my two children attended, and still we never spoke, we passed each other on our way. Eventually, as our children started to play together, we started to chat. I remember a conversation we had, I mentioned I remembered her from year's back, only to discover she wasn't the same person. Not that I thought badly of the person I assumed she was but imagine if it had been that way. Imagine if I had created this scenario in my head that she was someone else, who I had not got along with. Imagine if I had played that scenario out in my head, then discovered that she was this person. As it happened, she turned out to be a distant cousin on my Nan's side.

Making a mistake based on an assumption or judging someone on who you think they are and not who they are, could happen to anyone. You may easily mistake someone for a person they are not and start to gossip about them with unkind words and malice. Previously, I said never judge someone who you don't know, for they may not be who you think they are. Take advice from others and listen to your intuition, whether you believe their words to be true and let your head and heart guide you. Your intuition is that knowing feeling that you develop over time. It is developed through your accumulated wisdom, experiences, information and learning. You process and balance this using your logic and emotions, through what you think and what you feel. The more you experience in life, the stronger your intuition becomes.

When thinking of people, you used to know, you should recognise that they may be very different now to how they once were. They may have matured, developed and had life experiences that have shaped them into the person they are now. Think about how different you are now, from the person you used to be? Are you different, in a better way? Are there still ways in which you need to change? So before judging someone on what you think you know, or what you have heard, take a moment, be mindful, and think before you judge.

Taking Care of Yourself

There are times when you may forget to take care of yourself. You live in a society where you are almost forced to keep going but in reality, you can't. Unless you are kind to your bodies, they will eventually stop being kind to you. Your body may not reveal many problems to begin but slowly, bit by bit, your body will start to fall apart and as with most things, prevention is better than cure. *"If you consciously let your body take care of you, it will become your greatest ally and trusted partner" Deepak Chopra (Twitter.com, 2017).* When you listen to your body, it will show you what is going on and what needs to change.

How many times have you craved something to eat? Were you hungry? Feeling hungry is often a sign of dehydration. When you feel hungry, is it because you haven't eaten for a while or is your body playing tricks on you? For instance, is there an underlying problem about to surface? Gastritis can make you feel hungry when you are not. It often causes a burning sensation, indigestion or pain in the stomach, normally localised towards the left-hand side.

A craving for food that you may not even be fond of may be an indication of a deficiency in certain vitamins or minerals. Have you craved foods so much and then eaten them and felt worse afterwards? A good illustration is when you visit a bakery and smell freshly baked bread, pastries and cakes. Recall the warm scents wafting silently through the air to stimulate your nasal senses. Your taste buds become excited and you are sorely tempted to buy something; with high expectations of the delicious, aromatic and comforting tastes. However, having eaten them you discover, your stomach starts to bloat, you feel full and uncomfortable and lethargy starts to kick in.

The pleasant smells no longer appeal and the overwhelming feeling now is discomfort and possibly nausea. Alcohol is another thing that tempts many of you. Not always through the smell of a drink but often through the encouragement of others through social drinking or a desire for the relaxed state that the sedative affect of drinking may create. Your mood maybe lifted and your inhibitions reduced, but these effects are short lived, and soon wear off; possibly leaving you feeling anxious, upset, tired, sick, irrational and unwell.

What your body sometimes craves and what you think will make you feel good at the time, won't necessarily be any good for you later. So, take good care of yourself, incorporate self-love and wisdom in your choices, start to be kind to your body and your body will be kind to you.

Accepting Yourself

The things you read, see and hear in the media can have a powerful effect on you, both good and bad. You may find yourself in a moment of envy and idealism that puts you off balance, where you end up yearning to be someone or something you are not. You may even find it difficult to accept yourself for who you are.

There may be times when you wish you had someone else's life. You may idealise someone to the extent that you want the other person's look, skin colour, figure, wealth, partner, fame or more. But how much do you want this? Do you understand the consequences of having this? For a start, it's impossible to be another person, other than yourself. You are who you are.

If you start to nurture thoughts of being another person, ask yourself what it is about that person that you like? Is it their figure? Well, let's start by looking at your own figure in the mirror and see what it is about this that you don't like. You don't have to be too critical here. If what you don't like about yourself is your body size, be realistic about this. An underlying condition may make it difficult to lose or gain weight, such as diabetes, an autoimmune condition, like an under or overactive thyroid or lymphedema that causes swelling of the lymph glands and retention of fluid. Do you have issues with your legs, that make walking a problem? Before you move away from the mirror, look yourself in the eye and make a positive affirmation to yourself about what you like about you, and repeat this affirmation many times.

Bear in mind that if the person you want to be like is a celebrity who is in the limelight, most of the time, they are there to look good and please others. They probably hire or are given hair and make-up stylists for all public appearances and possibly have their photos airbrushed or photo-shopped. They may hire a personal trainer for regular, one to one exercise training to keep them looking in top physical shape. So, don't assume they are naturally the way you see them.

Coming back to your body shape and size, most of you must work hard to stay focused on losing weight and maintaining your shape; not to mention finding the time to do so. What is it that stops you from losing or gaining weight? Is it because you feel you have already tried every diet there is? How long did you try each diet? Did you give up after the first few days or weeks, or did you complete them, before deciding they did not work for you? Maybe it was the type of diet you chose. In reality, you don't have to go on a diet at all. Being more selective about the types of food you eat, having smaller portion sizes, drinking more filtered water, cellular-cleansing and taking regular, active exercise if possible will help you to lose weight and with a positive and disciplined mindset, will ensure you keep extra weight off.

Do you exercise? As you are probably already aware, exercise is good for you, especially in helping to improve your shape, figure or muscle tone. But it is just as good in helping to improve our mood and outlook, by releasing endorphins and other neuro transmitters. If a disability restricts what you can do, there are many exercises that can be done sitting or lying down. For others there are standing exercises, walking, running and swimming to name a few. So, don't allow yourself to create barriers that prevent you from doing something about this, as doing nothing will keep you in the body in which you currently reside.

Coming back to the previous affirmation I asked you to do; look again at yourself in the mirror and tell yourself that you are beautiful, you are amazing. Tell yourself you are anticipating a journey of losing or gaining weight, that you will do so in a way that helps you to stay focussed on your health goals, creating a more determined and energised you, who radiates beauty from inside out.

Is it their wealth that you find appealing? Do you know how they acquired their fortune? Unless they won the lottery, it would not have come to them overnight. What stops you from working to make more money? What things do you need to change to make your life more financially secure? If you had the amount of money that they have, what would you do with it? How sensible would you be with it? Would you invest it wisely, or would it all be gone too soon?

Is it their partner that you desire? What is it about that person that you like? Are you in a relationship? If you are, are you unhappy with your partner? If you are not, is it that you would like your future partner to be like them?

You know you cannot have that person. But you can set yourself standards for how you would like your next partner to be to make you happy. If it's a current relationship and your partner has habits or behaviours that you do not like, speak to them honestly about these, as no relationship works without good communication. You never know until you talk about things. Your partner may be willing to make changes for the growth and longevity of your relationship, and likely; you may have to make some changes too. In a future partner, you may find all or only some of those standards and may need to compromise on the rest. You may find that when you are in a relationship your 'ideal' for what you wanted in a partner may not be that important in the end.

Think more deeply before you act. Your life may be far from the ideal and perfection you desire, but it might be those areas of imperfection, that inspire, motivate and help you keep a positive outlook on life. The reality of having someone else's life is very different to having that life. What may seem ideal on the outside is not always the case on the inside. Flip the coin. You may have positive things about your life that they do not have and would like, which you have not even considered, in your current mind-set of wanting to be like them. You may have a happy and stable family life and a strong network of friends who support you. You may have talents you do not fully use. You can change, and grow, to use your talents and abilities to their full potential. This is how you will get to where you want to be in life.

Self-Worth

Everyone loses things in life. What have you lost today? Your keys, your phone, your wallet or purse, your voice, your friends, your family, your dignity, your self-worth or your self-respect? How important was, what you lost? Is it replaceable like your keys? Is it something intangible and much harder to replace, like your self-worth? What's important to you right now and how can you replace what you have lost?

Keep your self-worth subjective and positive, value yourself for what you are worth, don't allow yourself to fall short of your abilities and potential, surround yourself with kind, loving and respectable people.

Failings and Successes

My failings are my future successes. Failing is part of your healthy growth, and learning is a stepping stone to success for those who are motivated to achieve their goals. For many of you, your success was not always present and came from failing, not once or twice but many more times. You must keep your eyes on the prize, keep going, learning and growing. You have achieved your success through the lessons life has taught you. *"Past thoughts equal' present behaviour" "You don't make decisions on what's happening, you always do it based on what's happened before, so you're always doing things based upon past knowledge" Denis Waitley (Abundance-And-Happiness. Com, 2017)*

Don't be too hard on yourself if you fail. Sometimes failing is an acceptable option, as you develop great courage, enthusiasm and determination. Whoever said that success has to happen? Failing evokes strong emotions that you often internalise; attributing blame to yourself for failing to understand how life constantly changes, failing to understand other's and their feelings—so through blame that you take on, your emotions are expressed through frustration, misunderstanding and often by throwing in the towel.

Some aspects of failure are easier to see, such as in business. If the customers don't come, if profits are marginal or non-existent, then wages cannot be paid, if the business collapses within the first two years. When all is said and done, keep an open mind about things and be willing to keep trying.

You must go on many journeys to achieve your goals; you must understand life to experience its offerings. It's only when you have witnessed the darkness that you understand the light. So, don't give up. There may be many steps you need to take. Those steps may have to be small, before you can take bigger ones. Stick with the process you are trying but accept that if it's not working, you must try something else. So, have a contingency plan. Be completely open to learning from experience. Analyse the reasons why your business or project failed. Were there forces outside your control—things that you had no control over and were unable to change? If it was within your control, look at what you need to change next time around. One thing for certain is if you do give up you will never have success.

Don't ever be too hard on yourself; some things won't work out the way you want. *"I'm as good as the best but not better than the rest." Denis Waitley (Mindvalley)*

You must get to this point to expand, to learn, to grow. So, find a way to make it to the end. If you, remain totally focused on what you want, are disciplined and never give up despite problems and setbacks, you will be on the path to success and abundance.

Keep Calm

You don't always see what's staring you in the face. Have you noticed that when you are stressed or erratic, you cannot find what you are looking for? It could be a simple email you can't locate when it is there on your screen. How many times have you lost your keys, only to realise they're on the table or the sofa next to you. Sometimes they fall between the sofa cushions; it's amazing what lurks inside those gaps. When your erratic, panicky mind is engaged, the likelihood of finding what you want in a hurry, quickly diminishes. It may take you some time to find what you've lost; you may look in the same place several times but are still unable to find it. Then you go back to the first place you looked and there it is, as if someone has sneaked up and put it there, but I assure you they haven't—it's to do with your busy mind. When you are in this state, you are unable to see what is in front of you causing your stress levels to increase. Once you stabilise and calm your mind, then you normally find what you were looking for.

You see most of the time the things you think are lost, are not lost at all, they are exactly where you left them. But until you take a moment to calm your breathing, to still your erratic mind, you cannot think logically or clearly. Instead you go into a panic and worry state and it snowballs from here. It starts off with lost keys, then a panic of being late. When you still can't find your keys, the panic of being late for work, to not getting to work at all gets worse. If not found, feelings of guilt follow—all the people you will let down, customers, co-workers and your boss. It advances to the (irrational) fear of not getting paid. It all seems like a soap opera, but that's because this has probably happened to everyone. *"I am always good at losing things, even though those things are in front of me." —Donella Hoyle, July 2017*

The reality is that you all know this is preventable. Preparation is the key (sorry for the pun). New routines are needed to remove old habits that don't serve you well. So, with keys in tow on the day, hour, or moment before you need them, put them in a dedicated place where you know how to find them every time, such as a key rack. If someone else uses them, don't panic. Ask where they put them, chances are they know. If not, calmly go through the following questions. When did you last use them? Where do you think they are likely to be? Where were you last, when you had them? Hopefully, you will have located them after the first question, but if not stay calm until you find them. Now you can use this simple questioning technique on yourself if you lose anything in the future—other than your keys (as you know where they are now, right). With a calm state of mind, this approach will prevent a scenario like this in the future.

Similarities

Have you ever spoken to someone, who reminds you of someone else you know? Maybe you found their similarities uncanny. It may have nothing to do with their looks but more to do with their behaviour. But have you ever thought of looking beyond this, past their personalities to sense their energies instead? For as you already know you are all energy beings, although your energies might not be on the same level as others.

As your lives become more harmonious, you will tend to stop looking at people's differences in social or economic status, religion, colour, ethnicity or sexual orientation. Instead you will look at your shared values and experiences. You realise that after all the exterior is stripped away, everyone is a human. You all need, to experience life and to serve. Maybe in a world where everyone looked and sounded the same, acceptance would not be questioned. However, as everyone is different; in their looks, what they wear and their experiences this makes it a diverse and beautiful thing and needs to be embraced. Imagine how dreadfully dull life would be if everyone behaved and looked the same.

Sometimes you may analyse people based on how they look, even if they have not uttered a word. Take some of the popular TV talent shows in recent years, they have showcased many amazing singers, some of whom on first appearance, may have presented themselves poorly. Assumptions are quickly made; you may already have judged the person on their appearance, not their ability to sing, which you have yet to hear. When they sing, the harmonic and beautiful sounds cascading from their mouths, leaves you spellbound, not least as you have already judged them.

You can all find someone attractive because of their persona, the way they dress, the way they look, but when their energy comes through it can change how you feel about that person. I know as I have experienced this myself so many times before—when you think a person seems like someone else you know until their true character emerges. When a person has unpleasant characteristics, the exterior mask cannot stay on forever.

CHAPTER SIX

Mind, Body and Spirit

Beautiful Beings

Thomas Overbury, an English poet, is known for the famous saying "beauty is only skin deep," and this has an element of truth. The society we live in over emphasises the importance of superficial beauty, superficial politeness, and superficial kindness—all rather skin deep. How aesthetically pleasing to the eye you are, how well presented you are, how the contours of your face lie, how young you may look for your age, how slim you are, how charming or enchanting you are; may be important attributes. But are they as important as internal qualities of integrity, honesty, faithfulness, selflessness, generosity, compassion and caring? There are many whose beauty exudes from within, and irrespective of our sometimes, culture-bound standards of external beauty, they cannot be denied this.

Inner beauty often radiates like warm energy, from a person with a kind, generous and caring nature. On the other hand, superficially beautiful people may be very appealing to look at but, like the mythical creature Medusa, one look from them could turn you to stone (metaphorically speaking), for on the inside there is nothing good. Appearances as you all know can be deceptive.

What does beauty mean to you? Is it, skin deep only? Is it the external beauty with superficial mannerisms or is it simply the internal qualities that are shown when it comes to helping and caring for others in this world, where your mission is to serve?

Over time perceptions of physical beauty have changed. Across the world, ever evolving cultures see different things as beautiful. What is beautiful in one setting may not be regarded as beautiful in others. Tattoos, piercings, make-up, plastic surgery, skin lightening, skin tanning, facial hair or no facial hair. As I see it, the real test of beauty is in how beautiful your character and nature is as a person—how you serve others, how you radiate this inner beauty so others can see that you have a beautiful soul.

As you continue your journey through this book, you will start to look at things at a deeper level and find out how beauty can radiate from anyone who is genuine, shows integrity, kindness, love, generosity and acts selflessly. Those who possess these qualities transform themselves into attractive and beautiful beings that draw others to them in a way that those who are superficial never could. Mother Theresa and Gandhi are examples of people renowned for the beautiful things they did for others.

Beauty as I understand it is what defines a person as being happy and loving. They are confident and comfortable in themselves. Beauty is an experience that can be witnessed with the eyes through a person's behaviour and characteristics. Beauty is the mystique a person holds, the pleasure in one's eye, the experience of love, kindness, and desire. This experience of beauty is far more appealing than external beauty.

It is a lasting beauty that continues to grow with the person the more beautiful that person becomes inside.

There is no harm in looking your best for any given situation; in fact, I would encourage this, as long as you are happy with it. Never feel pressured into pleasing others unless it pleases you, as resentment can arise. Feel comfortable in yourself. Be proud of who you are, how you look and how you feel.

Some days you will feel tired. This tiredness may affect your body and mood, so try to find ways to give yourself a boost. Looking better on the outside can have a positive effect on how you feel on the inside. So, I have included a lovely scrub below, to help remove impurities and toxins from your skin to make you glow and feel restored, and another relaxing meditation exercise.

Home-Made Sugar Scrub

Use half a cup of coconut or olive oil, half a cup of salt or sugar and a few drops of essential oils, such as lavender, rose or other that takes your preference. Be cautious of citrus oils such as Bergamot, Lemon, Lime, Orange and so forth as sun exposure and ultra violet light will cause the skin to become photosensitive and is likely to damage or burn the skin.

Then mix all your ingredients together, store in an airtight jar and enjoy.

When making the scrub, as mentioned above some oils react to the sun and this will continue during storage. Opt for a coloured jar such as blue, brown or green instead of the clear type as exposure to sunlight may cause the product to react. Use the scrub once a week until you have used it up.

Afterwards apply moisturiser directly to your face and body to restore, repair and rejuvenate your skin.

Meditation Seven: Relaxation Time

Its summer outside and as you venture out, you feel how warm the day is, with a breeze so gentle it softly caresses your skin. It's very peaceful here with only the sounds of nature in the background. You look up to the sky, and the clouds layer it with white streams floating along as the Earth orbits the sun.

As you look higher into the sky you see a flock of swallows circulating in a pattern, they then merge before flying apart. I want you to now imagine you are one of these birds flying high with your wings stretched out, gliding through the air. With each gust of wind, you find yourself moving faster. You hear the other birds calling, so you fly in their direction, each of you putting on a fine display of your aerodynamic agility. When it's your turn, you fly towards the others and swoop, your head down, then using your ability you push up into a straight line above you. When you reach your vertical peak for this display, you twist around falling slowly down almost floating and then hover over a spot balancing your body in mid-air. Your ego never took over in this display nor did it ever show its face, but instead you were there for demonstrational purposes so that others can learn and grow in themselves.

So let the teacher in you flourish, serve others in a way that allows them to achieve the best of their ability knowing that the first step to becoming happy and fulfilled in life, is to make others happy too. Continue your own journey in the sky, gracing it with your presence. Fly with the freedom that you always had, learning from others, and teaching on the way, knowing that like the bird, nothing can ever control you. Don't try to control your moments, your thoughts, your feelings, or your life; be free, as free as a bird.

Meditation Eight. How Colour Affects Our Lives

We are drawn to colour in our lives more than we know, for most of us never see the world in black and white. The colour we see is based on how a pigment absorbs and reflects the light. When light hits an object, some is absorbed, and some is reflected. Our eyes perceive the reflected portion as colour. It was once thought that animals such as cats and dogs only see in black and white, but this is only a myth, as they also see in colour. However, they don't see as many colours as humans.

What would life be like, if everything lost its colour? We would no longer see flowers in the same way for their brilliant range of colours is a way of attracting pollinators, such as bees.

The colours of the flowers help to target the areas of nectar. That's the reason why petals are usually a different colour than the leaves. Even though humans can see more colours, bees have a much broader range of colour vision. They can see ultraviolet light, and this gives them an advantage when seeking nectar. Many patterns found on flowers are invisible to human eyes.

If we were to see one object in colour against a black and white background whether this object is moving or motionless we are instantly drawn to this, for colour plays such an important part in our lives. We are born without being able to see properly. Initially, we can only detect light and motion before we start to distinguish faces and large shapes. As our brain develops so does our ability to see more clearly. We go from being able to see objects near to moving objects.

When colour is ever present in our lives, our moods tend to react to the rainbow of brilliance. Light colours such as whites and blues may help to still our mind and calm our *wellbeing, but too much blue may give us the blues. Reds may evoke a fire within us, a determination and passion. Blacks may make us feel sad or down in the dumps. Yellows such as the colour of the sun may restore our moods, making us feel alive with more energy and vibrancy than before. A mixture of colours swirling together may make us feel queasy or raise our blood pressure.*

So, try to imagine a scene now where colour is present such as a golden sandy beach with its grains of sand and its brilliant blue waters. Look out to the sea and see a pure white sailing boat drifting slowly on the waters. See a woman standing on the boat with her decadent red swimwear and her black raven hair, blowing gently in the wind. As you look up, you see a flock of starlings flying in the sky with their brown bodies as rich as warm chocolate and purple and green necks, yellow beaks and orange legs as bright as a blazing fire. How many other colours can you see? Are there many more colours that your eyes see in this scene that you have created? Become more aware of colour in your life now and what an important role it has in your outlook for the day.

CHAPTER SEVEN

Unwanted Thoughts

Life can be stressful with its ups and downs. When these get the better of you, it can lead to unpleasant and unwanted thoughts that are obtrusive, obsessive and unpleasant. They may be caused by anxiety, fear, anger, jealousy, hate, and depression.

These unwanted thoughts are not of a balanced mind. They draw you away from the light, away from hope and into your darker selves; the darkness of your soul. You can only get back to the light, by confronting the dark; the darkness that holds your doubts, fears, negative beliefs, pain, grief and sadness.

Dark Moments

Dark moments,
Dark times,
Death is what will face me.
My head is filled with the strain from the clutter that fills
my mind.
Like Bees hurrying around their Queen,
The demons within me eating at my flesh and my soul.

—Donella Hoyle, January 2017

You did not become a light being by staying in the light, but by pulling yourself out of experiences in the dark that threatened to consume you and through this, making your way back towards the light. The light is your answer to all the energy that is, for energy is what made you who you are.

So, when your thoughts focus on your unhappiness and draw you back to this darkness, you may recall negative events and feelings and reflect on all that you don't like, what you wish was different and what caused you pain and suffering. But by holding onto unhappy thoughts and dwelling on the past, you create more unhappiness and more darkness. You know you can pull yourself clear of this and remind yourself of where you are and who you have become. When you are mindful and focus on the present, you see the past as a way to move forward, not to look back. The past is what made you who you are now and what you will become.

From this balanced perspective, you can observe the negativity in other people, and you can find your positive attributes. See the unwanted behaviours of others, as a way to reinforce and appreciate the positive things about yourself.

Letting Go of the Negative

When you have a thought that is negative teach yourself to discard it so that negative thoughts are passed by as quickly as they come. Develop a habit of telling the unwanted thoughts to go away. Practice this, and it will become a good discipline to help you. As you learn to address these thoughts carefully, deep down you will also know your mind, and learn to distinguish between your internal voice and one of a higher-self, guardian angel or spirit.

Focus on the good feelings in your life. Everything else, including unkind thoughts about others, draws in negative energy that causes stagnation in your mind and body.

Re-focus your thoughts on something positive or visualise yourself creating a bubble and placing all these unwanted thoughts and feelings inside it, then gently blow the bubble away. Continue to watch this bubble disappearing in your mind's eye and with it feel the release of the stale negative energy moving away from your body, as it is no longer wanted.

Sometimes your mind or the Universe will test you, to see how far you will go to push aside negative thoughts that stand in your way. Some believe that negative thoughts are caused by evil spirits if you believe in spirits. In some religions, the Devil represents this evil spirit or fallen angel. Others see negative thoughts as positive and negative energy like that of the Chinese philosophy of Yin and Yang.

Good spirits, such as your spiritual guides and angels, will try to communicate with you at times to offer guidance, but there will also be bad spirits too. Let's take the word Devil and look at it in more detail. By reversing the word, it becomes 'lived.' So, like the negative thoughts that you have, you can change them so that they become positive and uplifting.

When life is getting you down, take a break. Don't be too hard on yourself. Sometimes you place too many expectations on yourself, and things don't always go the way you expect. When this happens, you feel deflated and disappointed in yourself, which decreases your use of positive energy and instead consumes negative energy. This feeling can shift the way you are into a negative way of thinking.

Practice meditating when you can, it helps, put life into perspective. It is a proven way to quiet the mind and slow the heart. Through this practice you can energise yourself, attracting higher vibrations, allowing the positive energy to flow freely through your energy centres in your bodies, known by many as your Chakras. I write more about these later in the book.

Letting Go

You have all probably experienced battles in life. Some of you more than once and that's not to say you won't have more battles on the way. It's how you deal with these battles that matter most. When you were a child or teenager, these battles may have devastated you perhaps causing you to grow up too quickly and affected you into adulthood. Battles in adulthood can be as traumatic, but it's harder to deal with negative experiences when you are young, as the warrior in you hasn't yet grown to its strongest form. Some of you may carry bad memories, thoughts, and feelings from childhood, into adulthood.

So, what can you do about this? If you're reading this book now and have suffered any kind of trauma, then you have already overcome part of the obstacle that you have faced.

The exercise below will take you through steps to help you release blockages in your life.

Releasing Your Blockages:

Thinking about the problem, incident or situation that happened (this could be a painful or uncomfortable experience, but please let's try and face this together in this chapter, for now, you need to know you are not alone). You do not need to spend too long on this but let's take it from the beginning.

What was it that happened?
How did it affect you in the way it did?
How did you deal with it?
Did you confront the situation, or did you move the thoughts to the back of your mind?
Was there some physical or mental trauma that's still there, present in your mind?

So now that you have gone through this part you know the following:
1: What the problem, situation or battle is.
2: You understand how you have dealt with this or suppressed it.
3: You also know if the situation was right or wrong, good or bad.
4: You recognise that you are not alone to deal with this, we are on this journey together and there are so many people, friends, families, and organisations that can help you too, so reach out to them as and when you need them. (At the end of this book are contact details for organisations that provide help).

You now have the necessary information, which you may have known already. If something new has come to the surface as you went through the events, it may be that you had previously suppressed it.

Now together let us try to minimise the hurt, pain or suffering you felt, or still feel.

Looking at the situation do you see who or what was involved? Hopefully, you can. If not, don't worry.

Grab a pen and some paper and write down the people, group, and organisation whatever it may be, as a number or letter, for example, if it was a person use the initial of their first name. Do this, until you have it all listed clearly.

Now, look at each number or letter that you have given each person or group, etc. Start with the first and move down. See what it is about that number/letter that made you suffer, feel inadequate, uncomfortable, unhappy or any other thoughts or feelings evoked here.

Write down your thoughts and feelings or be somewhere where you can be vocal. Give it a voice, the sound to be heard. Speak or shout aloud to project your thoughts outwards until you feel the negative energies that caused this, disappearing with your exhalation. If you cannot speak aloud, say them in your head and try to feel the same emotional release as speaking out loud.

Eradicating these thoughts and feelings from your body, mind, and soul should eliminate your suffering. You've held onto this for too long.

Once you feel you have said or written down what you need to deal with, I want you to feel like you can forgive that number/letter. Be mindful, this could be a difficult thing in the beginning, but it is a powerful and important part of the healing process that you need to go through. Re-facing the trauma and acknowledging it, before you let it go, frees you from this and brings about release on an emotional and psychological level.

See the moment you are in bringing warm energy and healing to your body from inside out. See that number/letter as someone who like you may have previously suffered from a problem, crisis, unhappy lifestyle, abusive relationship or background. Try to understand that like you, those that caused you this suffering might never have known how to deal with it in the right way and so dealt with it by causing you pain. Now you are wiser and removing the negative feelings attached to this experience; I want you to replace these thoughts with positive ones, thoughts where you bring inner strength to your mind and body.

Use past negative experiences as lessons to help yourself and others, who like you may also have suffered, rather than negative thoughts to dwell. Use them now to teach others to grow strong like you have, to show them the way forward, to be a hand when they need one to hold, to be the ears when they need someone to listen.

No longer should anyone suffer pain, in this way. Help them to see their experiences as their catalyst to change to do good, to improve their lives, to be someone they never thought they could be—a listener, teacher, mentor, a supportive and empathic person that people look to for positive change and growth for the greater good.

You may have to undertake this exercise more than once, so repeat as little or as often as necessary. The more you face your fears, the more battles you will win. Trauma has no place in controlling you, or the power to hold onto you anymore. Pain affects you mentally, emotionally, physically and spiritually and can put you out of balance. Holding onto your pain will create further difficulties that keep you connected to the trauma. By realising them, you start to release the ties or attachment that they had on you.

The process of healing in this way is a personal one; a process that brings inner strength and growth, to help you go forward and not hold you back. No longer does 'flight' in our "Fight or Flight" response apply to you, for now, you can stand tall because you have fought and are now grounded to the earth.

Practice the Yoga Tree pose to ground your feet to the Earth like the roots of the tree. Feel your arms stretching out to the sides like branches of the tree, then bring them into the

heart in a prayer position. Then stretch them up way above your head. Elongate your spine towards the sky, like a tree trunk reaching up towards the sun and stand firm as you feel your feet grounded to the floor like the roots of a tree to help reconnect you to the Earth.

I would now like you to undertake a meditation, which can help with this healing process. Before you do this, I want you to, think of the thing, person or event that affected you and add it, after the word forgive.

Meditation Nine: Releasing

I choose to forgive .... for the pain/suffering/trauma I have experienced, but no longer will I be a victim of this. I am a strong warrior ready to show my courage and strength. As a warrior, who wins the battle now and from this day forward, I am healing and restoring my positive ways of thinking and mindset. I will show only compassion as I can now be the best me, and I will act to bring this about. For I will no longer allow these emotions to control me, I will no longer be the victim of my suffering, I have grown and will continue to grow, heal and be painfree from this trauma forever more.

Awakening

At some point in your life, you may experience what is known as a spiritual crisis. A spiritual crisis could be a time when things seem to keep going wrong. No matter what you try, instead of things coming together, they fall apart. My advice is to have patience. Practicing patience may be easier said than done when faced with a situation, but patience brings wonderful experiences that you may not be expecting. You may start to see that what you are experiencing may not be as bad as it first seemed. In fact, it could be the complete opposite, and what you are experiencing could be your awakening.

Sometimes it may take you a while, to realise between a moment and a day, exactly where your life is going. Some may feel that their life doesn't go anywhere but drifts along. Then, out of nowhere, an experience like a tidal wave can strike you, with waves crashing over you with an almighty force. The feeling of the wave is like a catastrophic, explosive whiplash. Fear not though, for this is your life playing itself out before you so that you can take the time to observe what is happening.

The moments, days, weeks and months that you are facing are here now to wake you up, to shake you up, into a newly conscious and profound person. You pull yourself out of this dreamy state of mind, to a greater spiritual awareness, that no longer sees everything as black and white, and looks beyond all which you have known before. Change now occurs, without resistance. Like the circle of life, you were born, you live, and you die, but it's all the in-betweens that you must experience first to reach fulfilment.

See yourself as a new person who forgives themselves for the past. The past has now gone and cannot be changed. A new person will forgive themselves for those all too familiar moments when their mind was unbalanced and they lacked wisdom. See yourself as a new person with an improved state of being, where you finally see that you have learnt so much, come so far, and are becoming wiser through your experiences.

If you are faced with these experiences again, you know you will have a wholly different experience. You will carefully think before you act, and you will know your inactions have consequences, and your wrong actions have regrets. So, with your new-found changes, you will discover that you have finally woken up.

"Success is to be measured not so much by the position one has reached in life, as by the obstacles which he has overcome"

—Booker T. Washington (Literaturepage.com, 2017)

Believe in yourself and those around you will believe in you.

—Donella Hoyle, January 2016

The Shift and Signs to Look for

The shift is the transformation from your present consciousness to your higher self, towards a greater spiritual awakening that brings about a sense of peace, calm and unity.

When the shift occurs listen to your body and think about how it feels, you will become aware of pain in a much different way than before. Deeper spiritual growth can bring about subtle awakenings in your body, which are often a very disconcerting and distracting transition.

With my personal pain comes my acknowledgement of too many responsibilities weighing on my shoulders. Pain travelling up my back causes a misalignment in my neck. My throat protrudes forward creating a curvature in the back of my neck. Through this body conscious process and physical experience, my body tells me that something needs to change to get true body and soul realignment. My throat protrudes in this way to make me aware that something needs to be spoken for inner healing and spiritual development to take place. To allow my body to rid itself of negative energy and feelings and make way for free-flowing positive energy, to bring back strength, clarity and total body alignment.

When you are in this transitional state, your mind may wander, and your thoughts may be in disarray. You need to act on this emotional change and open up to this spiritual awareness that maybe you were not interested in before.

Listen to your body and feel the physical connection, as

you let go of your ego, putting new purpose and meaning into your life. Understand that you may need to experience your darkest moments to face light—to create change by observing yourself meeting with your spiritual side so that you can surrender to this transition rather than giving into to the controlled state that you have become so accustomed to.

I found that through being weak, I grew to be strong again. This may sound contrary, but it's true. When I suffered low points in life, and I hit rock bottom or close to it, I started to feel a change. I felt, something positive lifting my spirits, something I may not have thought about or realised before came to me and finally started to shift. So be patient, and it may also come to you.

It may occur like a soft and gentle breeze when something in you starts to stir, something in you wants and needs to change. It may hit you like a lightning bolt, striking you down from the skies above, (metaphorically speaking). But when it does, embrace it, for it will pick you up from that dark, lonely point in your life, where your self-worth is starting to vanish, when hope has almost faded. Finally, you get back to that point where you realise you do have strength left in your body and are gaining new strength. Don't waste this strength; use it wisely, so you feel alive. *"Nothing ever goes away until it teaches us what we need to know." Pema Chödrön (Goodreads. com, 2018).* So, face your fears and challenges rather than going against them.

Signs and How to See Them

I believe that you all have angels and spirit guides that provide you with signs throughout your day. Guidance from your angels come in many ways. You mostly dismiss them as coincidences or are afraid to admit they are signs. When you talk about signs, people are often unsure what they should be looking out for, but when you see one with an open mind, you will know. It may be in flowers, feathers, coins, numbers or names, but when words are not attached, be attentive so that you don't miss them. These signs are your connection to your birth angels. So, if something happens and you think it could be a sign, pay attention as it probably is.

Have you had moments when you think about someone you haven't seen in a while and then bump into them in the street? You hear the telephone ring, and before you lift the receiver you know who the call is from? You are drawn to a certain place, and the name of a street feels relevant to you in some way. You find feathers or coins that were not there before. You even see things that your mind tells you are improbable or impossible, but you know you saw them. Have you ever felt a tingly sensation down the side of your neck, when there is no wind, or heard a soft, loving and supportive voice in your head that you know is not yours? Have you ever been fortunate enough to avoid an accident, as your gut feeling told you to change direction?

Angels are with you 24/7. They support and guide you when you are in need; you only have to evoke them or ask for their help. They do so willingly. Some people have one angel others may have more, there is no specific number, but you are all born with an angel by your side waiting to guide you, advise you and reassure you when you ask. They communicate through a telepathic process and of course through signs. They like you to try and work things out for yourself the best you can, but they will help where they can or when they have been asked and will often send you signs, so pay attention.

Some people see signs on a daily basis but are so oblivious to what they see that they continue to go about their day as if they had seen nothing. There are those that notice things and pass them by. Some will see things that puzzle them whilst others will stop, take note and appreciate what they have been shown, for they know that it is a sign. They show gratitude for what they have experienced and know that it is for a reason. They know that this is one of many signs that they have experienced before and one of many yet to come. So, the next time you see, hear or smell something that you think was meant for you, give thanks, for you know it is one of support and love. Your angels are your soul's best friend, so never feel alone. Your angels have nothing but unconditional love for you, which binds you both together forever, so never be afraid to ask for help, they are always willingly waiting.

Mandalas

How do you spend your time relaxing? Some people read, some watch TV, some sit in the sun. How about getting your colouring pencils out and adding some colour to your book? I have included a Mandala here for you to colour in. Choose colours that are specific to you or make you feel happy.

A mandala according to Wikipedia is *"A mandala (Sanskrit: मण्डल, lit, circle) is a spiritual and ritual symbol in Hinduism and Buddhism, representing the universe.*[1] *In common use, "mandala" has become a generic term for any diagram, chart or geometric pattern that represents the cosmos metaphysically or symbolically; a microcosm of the universe". MANDALA (En. wikipedia.org, 2017).*

So, have fun with colouring this in or even draw your own. At the end of the book, I have included blank pages for your notes, drawings, and reflections, so you can refer to them as often as you choose.

CHAPTER EIGHT

Chakras

Chakras		Sanskrit Names
Crown		Sahasrara
Third Eye		Ajna
Throat		Vishuddhi
Heart		Anahata
Solar Plexus		Nabhi-Manipura
Sacral		Svadhisthana
Root		Muladhana

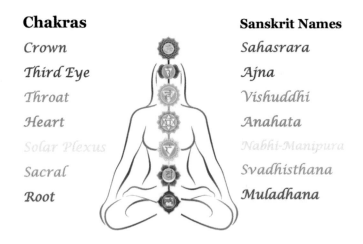

Chakras are the energy centres in the body. They are where your spiritual self, interfaces with your physical body. They are called Chakras, which in Sanskrit means spinning wheels of energy. The focus tends to be on seven chakras although there are many more. The seven you will be looking at here include; the Root chakra, associated with the colour red; Sacral chakra, associated with the colour orange; Solar plexus chakra, associated with the colour yellow; Heart chakra, associated with the colour green; Throat chakra, associated with the colour blue; Third Eye chakra, associated with the colour indigo and finally, the Crown chakra, associated with the colour violet or white. This seven-chakra system that is most familiar in the West is one of many and has been taught here since the 16th century.

Everything that I have covered in the previous chapters on energies, positive mind-sets, values and behaviours, in one way or another is relevant for maintaining balance across the chakras. Your chakras exist as an invisible, dynamic energy system that works synergistically with your mind and body. An understanding of how these spinning wheels of energy function will help you to maintain your chakra 'health' and enhance the positive benefits to your health and wellbeing for keeping your chakras well balanced.

When you hold onto and suppress negative emotions—anger, hate, dishonesty, fear, envy, jealousy, shame, etc. your chakras may become blocked. Releasing your problems, through positive practices that create a connection with your mind and body, including yoga, meditation, and energy healing, can help unblock and rebalance your chakras bringing harmony back to your mind and body.

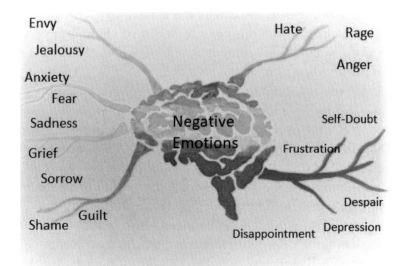

Seven Main Chakras

Root Chakra - *Muladhara*

This chakra is about your connection to Earth, your physical body and your connection to the chakras above it. It's about survival, the need for food, sleep, courage, power and the desire for self-preservation. It is at the base of your tailbone, so you sit on your root chakra. It is associated with your blood, skeleton, feet, legs, and teeth.

Problems with your root chakra can happen as early on as the birth process, especially in an unwanted pregnancy, and can continue throughout the successive stages of your lives. Trauma in the root chakra can develop into a mental or physical imbalance, fear or distrust of people. You may harbour thoughts of not belonging, become worried, stressed and distracted from life. When there is an imbalance in your root chakra, it affects the base of your spine and surrounding areas including legs and feet.

Sitting directly on the ground rather than on a cushion is a good way to connect to the earth, to ground yourself. Like the roots of a tree, you must feel the support of the earth beneath you and connect to the earth's electromagnetic energy and gain the benefit from this process. When you have grounded yourself, you will feel contented and safe knowing that your life is unfolding as it should.

To rebalance your root chakra, you need to release yourself from the past. Meditation, massage and reflective writing are practical ways to release past blockages. Eat root-vegetables, dance, sing, walk barefooted outside and hug a tree to reconnect and become one with nature.

Meditate and visualise the red light of your root chakra growing stronger. With each exhalation see the colour grow brighter, until you see a brilliant red burning flame. Useful crystals include Red Jasper, Smoky Quartz, and Hematite. Rosewood, Rosemary, Sandalwood, Black pepper, Cedar,

Cloves, and Ginger are earthy essential oils that are beneficial for healing.

Sacral Chakra - *Svadhisthana*

This chakra is about creativity, sensuality, passion, pleasure and your feelings. It influences your associations and interactions in your relationships with yourselves and others. In contrast to the security and grounding from your earth connection of the sacral chakra, the sacral chakra's association with water represents the more fluid and flexible flow of your emotions and feelings. Life cannot exist without water, and your body is comprised of around sixty percent water. Your sacral chakra is positioned in the pelvis around one to two inches below your navel. It is associated with your kidneys, bladder, reproductive system and genitals.

An imbalance in your sacral chakra can relate to addictions such as alcoholism, drug use, smoking, excessive sugar intake, caffeine, menstruation irregularities, urinary and bladder infections. Sexual behaviour may become dysfunctional and cause impotence, frigidity or promiscuity. Emotions such as anger, rage and resentment flow strong, when your sacral chakra is deficient, especially when you feel unappreciated, a failure and reflect too deeply on other people's opinions. These strong emotions left unchecked limit the flow of energy to your sacral chakra.

To rebalance your sacral chakra, try Yoga to open up the hip area, dance, and be satisfied with who you are. Head to the seaside and take a dip or wade in the water. Meditate and focus on seeing the vibrant orange of the sacral chakra as you release unwanted emotional baggage. Eat oranges, coconuts, and cinnamon to cleanse your body on the inside. Useful crystals include Carnelian, Citrine, Orange stones, and Moonstones.

Solar Plexus Chakra - *Nabhi-Manipura*

This chakra relates to your self-esteem, personal growth, your will and personal power. As named, it is in the solar plexus between the navel and sternum and is associated with your stomach, liver, pancreas, adrenal glands, lungs and digestive system.

When the solar plexus chakra is balanced, you are assertive, confident, think positively and deal with emotional issues in a positive way. You will have fun and feel at peace with yourself. You can look for ways to self-heal and protect yourself from illness. You will be free to serve others without expecting anything in return.

When out of balance you may have eating and stomach disorders, haemorrhoids, gallstones and hernias amongst other problems with the organs mentioned. Repressed emotions such as fear or grief may give rise to anger, and you may blame everyone else for your problems. You may find yourself becoming intolerant of others, overly competitive and controlling. You may turn to stimulants or relaxants where there is too little or too much energy in this area, but these will only mildly suppress, what are symptoms of an imbalanced solar plexus chakra.

Think about how you feel throughout the day, where are your peaks and troughs? Are you more of a morning person or better at night? What causes you to feel happy and energetic? And what merely makes you feel depleted?

To rebalance your solar plexus chakra, look for solutions by changing your diet, meditation, relaxing through reading, exercise such as walking and stretching. Reconnecting to the outside world and walking near rivers, lakes or the sea also help to stabilise and rebalance.

Heart Chakra - *Anahata*

This chakra lies in the middle of the seven chakras and is at the centre of your chest. It is where the physical meets the spiritual, where your emotions of love, warmth, and compassion emanate from and where your desire for harmony and peace are centred. Many eastern cultures see the heart chakra as the house of the soul. It is associated with your circulatory system, heart, lungs, thymus gland, arms, and hands.

When your heart chakra is imbalanced, you stop giving and receiving and this includes love and the need to be healthy. You may become unstable, uncaring and adopt unprincipled behaviours. Your emotions become entangled, and you cannot express your feelings, which shuts down your heart chakra and dims its light. At a physical level signs of a blocked heart chakra may show up as heart, lung and immune system problems.

The love you give out may have temporarily ceased due to a relationship that went wrong. Relationship issues may cause you to shut down your heart chakra to protect yourself, which results in more harm than good, for not only do you stop the love you give but you also stop love being received. Too much openness in the heart may cause excessive sacrifices to others and in doing so forgetting about your health and needs.

As with most things in life balance is key. When you meditate on your heart, you restore what is good and remove self-doubt, which causes sadness and may affect your posture, producing rounded shoulders that arise from your need for self-protection and preservation.

Imagine the green colour of the heart chakra becoming vibrant and pulsating with your heart's rhythm; see your heart reconnecting your mind, body, and spirit. Appreciate who you are. Start to love yourself again so that your heart energy can be restored and flow up towards your throat chakra. Consider what makes you feel loved and cherished, maybe it's the unconditional love of your pet, a soak in a hot bath with a face mask or the adoration of your children. Use incense of Jasmine or Lavender and have Rose Quartz crystals nearby to help put things back into place. You will restore balance as you eat more green fruit and vegetables.

Throat chakra - *Vishuddhi*

This chakra is the energy centre that allows communication to flow freely within you. It brings with it creativity, sound, self-expression, and voice. It is associated with your thyroid and parathyroid glands, neck, shoulders, arms, and hands. The throat chakra is where you connect and process creative thinking and ideas and speak your truth. It can be blocked through many things including, childhood experiences where you may have been told to be 'seen and not heard' and all those times when you yelled too much in arguments with your loved ones or when you shout at work colleagues in a noisy work environment. Have you gossiped too much or had a lisp or stutter? All these relate to blockages of your throat chakra.

An imbalance may appear through an inability to listen and communicate with others, such as excessive shyness, dishonesty, and blockage to your creative thinking. Illness may occur and cause throat problems and disorders, including thyroid problems. The throat may become swollen, making it difficult to speak, the neck may stiffen, muscles tighten, and causing pain and discomfort, even the mouth, teeth and jaw can be affected.

So, think about how you are as a person. Are you always self-editing what you say? Putting you under self-scrutiny; finding it difficult to speak at the correct tone or pitch, putting the rhythms of your throat chakra out of balance. When you speak, you should do so without, restraint, interruption or fear of how you sound and what you say.

Listen to others and offer guidance when it is necessary, what they say may be important and interesting. Make positive decisions using your inner voice to guide you along the way. See communication not as a way of life but as life itself.

To restore your throat chakra, try to resist lying, speak only the truth. Believe that what you say is of sound judgement that allows you to be creative and soulful with your thoughts and your words. Disengage with media, social networking and other news that is distracting and harmful to your way of thinking. Instead of listening to the long daily news on TV, maybe read or listen to updates sent to your phone. Censor what you read or listen to and absorb, keep it positive. Break away from old habits to let the quiet child or adult in you emerge as someone stronger, with a voice to be heard and respected. Let out your tears and let go of anger and guilt. Eat fresh fruit, use Turquoise crystals or wear as a necklace and burn Frankincense and Jasmine.

Third Eye - *Ajna*

This chakra is located between the eyebrows and behind the forehead and not related to a specific part of the body, where the previous chakras have been. The third eye is centred in the head, in the brain and is the control centre of the body. Your third eye chakra is about your intuition and psychic abilities, seeing your world in both a physical and spiritual sense. It helps guide and show you what is important.

Your third eye chakra comes with a high energy vibration as it governs your intellectual and intuitive abilities as well as developing your spiritual awareness. Nurturing your third eye chakra can help you think more clearly, improve your vision, perceive the subtle movement of energy, develop your imagination, connect to wisdom and arouse inspiration as well as creativity.

Your third eye chakra allows you to store information from past experiences and imagine the future. It connects you to your higher consciousness and to the higher realms that have no limits of time and space.

Through your third eye chakra, you experience life beyond all you have learnt and prepare yourself to ascend to an infinite source of knowledge and information about the past, present and the future.

When your third eye is blocked, your intuition is weak, and you may feel unsafe and distrust others. Your memory may become unreliable, and your eyesight can become poor, causing headaches and sinus problems. These problems make it difficult for you to visualise and create your goals, plans, and dreams and may cause nightmares, making you vulnerable to negative thoughts and feelings.

To restore balance, you need to re-energise your third eye chakra. You can do this first by grounding your base chakra. Using meditation, positive thinking and visualisation to create a successful outcome you listen to your psychic intuition to guide you correctly. Allow creative thoughts and feelings to re-energise and help release negative feelings, and fears and foster happiness, pleasure, and clarity in your lives.

Essential oils that can help restore balance are Saffron, Star of East, Lavender, and Rosemary. Ideal crystals include Amethyst or those of a similar colour to the chakra itself. When clearing your third eye chakra, you must be prepared to open your third eye. When doing so, you must protect yourself from psychic attacks—whilst meditating, imagine being surrounded by a purple cloak for protection. Take time for yourself, perhaps with a warm bath and candles to set a relaxed mood or take a walk somewhere that you can connect with nature. Honour and respect yourself and visit places that will re-energise rather than deplete your energy.

Crown Chakra - *Sahasrara*

This chakra relates to your spirituality and intuition connecting you to your thoughts and your consciousness or higher self and is located on the very top of your head, the very essence of your being. The crown chakra is associated with your pituitary and pineal glands and nervous system. As your root chakra connects you to the earth, allowing energy to flow into your chakras above, the crown chakra is your connection to the Universe, and it channels the universal energy down into all your chakras below. Tantric philosophy teaches that the crown chakra receives and gives energy and consciousness—universal energy is received to sustain life, which flows through you as your personal energy, uniting you with the collective consciousness.

Your crown chakra is about letting go of your Ego. You become aware that you are no more or less important than anyone else. You do not judge. You release the fixation on controlling your lives to determine specific outcomes—letting go of attachments and beliefs of a social, political, religious or economic nature that no longer support your enlightened self. When your crown chakra is balanced you experience a sense of peace, calm, enlightenment and positive energy will stream through you.

When too much energy is present in your lower chakras, it can create an imbalance in your crown and lead to dominating and controlling behaviours, greed, materialism, confusion, dizziness and mental fogginess.

Illnesses from an imbalance in your crown chakra are seen in the form of depression, epilepsy, headaches, mental illnesses, dementia, Alzheimer's and ADHD, to name a few.

The person with a dysfunctional crown chakra will appear arrogant and egotistical, where they have replaced their spiritual values with self-centred behaviours and a lack of belief in a higher power and consciousness. They think only about themselves and what they achieve.

To rebalance, you must reconnect with your spirituality to allow the energy to flow freely. You can strengthen, reopen and rebalance your crown chakra through meditation, relaxation, praying, chanting or other spiritual practices that help you to release your fears, stress, worry and your ego. When you accept that there is more than yourself, that you are part of a greater whole, you start to restore this balance. Having patience here will be rewarding.

Crystals such as Amethyst and Diamonds are useful for balancing, and Frankincense and Myrrh can be used for healing. Balance brings reconnection, and you realise that you are all connected to everyone and everything.

Meditation Ten: Chakra Meditation

Take some gentle breaths feeling the inhalation followed by and exhalation. As you relax a little deeper, start to focus your attention on your root chakra.

As you bring your awareness to your root chakra at the base of your tailbone, this emanates red light. It is associated with your connection to earth and your physical body, helping to ground you and enhance your energy. This is your sense of survival chakra that gives the will to live, the courage, the power, the desire for self-preservation. Fear or trauma in this area can develop into mental or physical imbalance. To rebalance this chakra, imagine this red light growing stronger with every inhalation. As the awareness continues up your spine towards your pelvis, this is your sacral chakra.

Take a moment to visualise the Sacral chakra's orange light, which when functioning properly is at its brightest. Is yours as bright as it should be or is it dimly lit? Let the colour grow in brightness as you see the orange blended from equal parts of red and yellow. This chakra relates to your emotions and offers us vitality and strength, giving us the desire for pleasure and to display talents and creativity. A lack of or too much energy in this area will create imbalance and dis-ease. With your inhalation restore this chakra; see the orange glow to its brightest.

Moving up, your third chakra located below your solar plexus is yellow in colour. It relates to your willpower, sense of belonging, self-esteem, and discipline. It is the core of your personality, your identity, and ego. As you become more aware of this colour and location - ask yourself if you have noticed any physical or emotional discomfort here.

Are there hobbies, interests that you need to work on, to develop further to grow or to slow down?

As you breathe in, see this yellow light becoming brighter as your personal drive grows or mellows, to rebalance the solar plexus.

Your next chakra is associated with your heart and the colour green or emerald. It symbolizes harmony, creativity, health, and abundance. It is an equal balance of the solar plexus yellow; relating to your soul and throat chakra blue; relating to your spirit.

Your heart chakra in its purest state is unconditional, unreserved and filled with joy. It represents love for each of us. It is about passion, taking time to appreciate things and feelings for others. But imbalanced, love can be associated with anger, distrust, and jealousy.

As you inhale allow your mind to let go of past relationships, beliefs, and experiences that may affect the way you love and trust yourself and others. With each breath, see this green light become brighter as you bring balance back to the very centre of your being.

Now moving up to your throat chakra, emanating a blue energy. This encourages spiritual communication and is linked to the throat, neck, arms, and hands. A balanced throat chakra is pure, soothing calming and healing. Is your blue light as vibrant as you want it to be? Is there something you need to say? Is there something you have said that you regret? Allow yourself the time to speak. If there's something you regret forgive yourself, as you rebalance your throat chakra and see your blue light becoming brighter.

Your next is your third eye chakra which connects to your sixth sense. Your third eye is between your brows. This indigo coloured chakra is linked to wisdom, higher knowledge, intuition, and an inner knowing. Your indigo light when shining brightly brings clarity to all your senses—hearing, seeing, feeling, tasting, and speaking. This chakra not only witnesses what you physically see but allows you to perceive *the meaning of what you witness. Allow yourself to reflect on whether you have been missing the obvious or seeing things where there are none. To rebalance here, allow your breath to bring about confidence and clarity. Feel the sensation between your brows as this happens.*

As we come to our final chakra, it hovers above our head. Our crown chakra has a purple or brilliant white light and allows you to transform the energy of lower chakras to higher spiritual vibrations. It connects you to the Universe; the Divine—that which is bigger than you, allowing you to be aware of your greater spiritual connection to all around you. If your life has become ungrounded and disconnected with friends and family, it can result in confusion, depression, and unhappiness.

As you inhale visualise a deep purple or white energy restoring balance and unity and as you exhale focus on restoring mind, body, and spirit. Let go of any feelings of disconnection and understand and appreciate how alignment feels.

Mind, Body, and Spirit

When you encourage your body and mind to work in accord and not opposition, you become attuned to how they work in synergy. You learn how to respond to the signals about your health and wellbeing when you are dealing with people and the affairs of your life. Chakra balancing meditation and spiritual practices help you to achieve this.

Become mindful, in the moment. Contrary to what the word implies 'mind-full' you are going to release your 'full' mind by allowing it to be in the present moment; the here and now. Your mind sometimes allows your thoughts to wander from being rational to irrational and you may have a habit of thinking about next week, month and even year, forgetting entirely about the present moment. When you become overly concerned with time and how little you have. Your balance is disrupted, and you plan your days away.

Take a clock face, with its numbers increasing in order and the hands set in the very centre. As you focus on the 'hands of time,' the seconds go by, turning to minutes, then hours. When you take your mind away from the moving hands of the clock, you go beyond the frame of time, as time itself starts to slow down, and you are no longer constrained by the time you have. By focusing your thoughts directly on the present moment, you become more aware of the physical aspects of your being. When you learn to slow down your breathing, your preoccupation with time is released. If you are distracted in the present moment, refocus on the inhalation and exhalation of your breath or the rhythmic beating of your heart.

Your heart is the largest organ in your body. It has physical and spiritual dimensions. The physical that you feel is the heartbeat, which you can measure with your pulse through your sense of touch. The spiritual cannot be measured in a way that any of your five senses can explain to you as it is non-physical, you cannot see it, hear it, touch it or smell it, nor speak it. Instead, you have a gut feeling, a sense of 'knowing,' a synergy of the physical and spiritual and an awareness of the energy you are formed of.

When you rest your bodies, and still your minds, your senses, slow down until they appear to stop. You still feel your heart beating, but more slowly, like a beacon of light. Now you can become more aware and attuned to the spirituality of your hearts, emanating through your body and you can open your heart to the divine that it is.

Through your spiritual growth and understanding that you are more than the physical body that you reside in, you soon become spiritually awakened. This 'awakening' tunes you in to receive and send messages, like a radio wave being transmitted, but at a frequency that not everyone will be ready to receive. This grounding happens on another spiritual plane when you have access to this dimension through a connection of energies that exist around and inside you and for those in search of the divine. Grounding helps you to connect to your truest self to communicate to your spiritual guides, angels and even the energy of those souls that have passed. This idea may be controversial for some people, but I am speaking from my own experiences. Your life starts to become more detached from possessions and become more attuned to a balanced, harmonious and conscious awakening. You become calmer, more alert and appreciative of how you experience life. This intensity opens your more sensitive and sensing abilities, which allow you to appreciate nature and its beauty that is often taken for granted. You become more present, mindful and conscious of a spiritual awakening in you.

When you become aware of who you are and what you are capable of, you can then understand that your mind, body, and spirit are not three separate things but are three things necessary to be one.

In chapter seven, I wrote about this shift in consciousness, as the transformation from your present consciousness towards a greater spiritual awakening that creates a sense of peace calm and unity.

Be the Best You

Do you believe in reincarnation?
Is this your only life or one of many?
One thing for certain is you are living life now.
So, use your life wisely,
Be the best you,
Be the most intelligent you.
But be true to you.

—Donella Hoyle, January 2017

Meditation Eleven: Mindfulness

We are often too distracted by our daily lives, focusing on many things at one time, instead of being present in the moment we are in. Distraction sometimes happens when we are driving along, and our mind goes into autopilot, a state called 'mindlessness.' In this busy modern world, we live in, we fill our lives with so much clutter and tasks to do that we completely forget about, simply being.

So, become aware of life in each moment, the thoughts and feelings, focusing on the here and now. Direct the attention to the present moment, don't become distracted by the past or the future. Be mindful in a non-judgemental state. Be aware of thoughts without trying to control them.

Every time you become aware of the present moment, the here and now, you are again in a mindful state.

Relax without expectations; disengage the mind from core beliefs that we experience fear in emotion. Go back to the root of the emotion and create the space it needs to be spoken, to be heard, to be, then release it, release it forever more.

Knowledge and Growth

A little knowledge is a dangerous thing if used in the wrong way. If the ego takes over, you may develop an overinflated opinion of your knowledge. This overinflated opinion will often lead to flawed ideas and inaccurate conclusions on the subjects in question. Alexander Pope had a great way of saying this in his poem, An Essay on Criticism in 1711; he wrote: *"For fools rush in where angels fear to tread" (En.wikipedia.org, 2018).* Having no knowledge at all can be riskier when you attempt to comment or inject your opinion on a subject that is not supported with evidence or experience.

However, having a broad range of knowledge is useful as some understanding on a range of subjects shows an appreciation for how things work or how people behave. When you keep an open mind and humble attitude it can help to show you where you need to continue to learn.

As this final chapter comes to an end, I hope that what you have read will open many more chapters in your life as you expand your personal growth and learning—to have a deeper understanding and appreciation of yourself and others, to value and forgive yourself, as you let go of emotional pain and replace it with joy and happiness, giving you greater enjoyment of life, and all it has to offer.

I sincerely hope I have challenged you in a way that has positively affected your life in the areas of this book that resonate with you. I hope that the array of resources provided will encourage you to take time out for yourself to relax, meditate and even indulge yourself occasionally, because you deserve it. More importantly, I hope I have whetted your appetite for a deeper knowledge towards your own spiritual enlightenment. Use this book for the purpose that it is intended, as a source for self-help whenever needed—this is a book to pick you up and not put you down.

Whilst I was writing this book I thought about how I would end it, even though I hadn't completed the middle, let alone imagined an ending. I thought this book would never need an end, because it can be re-read time and time again. Unlike our lives, we can go back and choose only the bits we enjoy.

If I have helped one person to feel alive and uplifted by reading this book, I believe that this positivity can spread further afield.

We can each have a positive impact on others. Sometimes it may seem insignificant. It may only take a smile, but if it lightens someone's life even for a short moment, then it is a job well done.

Thank you for reading my book, I hope you have enjoyed it. I wrote it to share parts of my life; my learning and my triumphs over challenges, great and small that have given me courage and determination. I hope it will offer guidance and support, whenever it is needed in your life so that you too, can continue your special journey.

This book has been a healing process, for the pen gave me my voice to communicate what my heart could not put into words.

—Donella Hoyle, November 2017.

Notes for Writing, Reflecting and Inspiring

Notes for Writing, Reflecting and Inspiring

Notes for Writing, Reflecting and Inspiring

Notes for Writing, Reflecting and Inspiring

Notes for Writing, Reflecting and Inspiring

You can find a range of health and wellbeing treatments, courses, videos, meditation downloads and more available at, www.transformyourlifewithdonella.com

Organisations That Can Offer Help and Support:

Samaritans
Tel No: 116 123
Or 0800 58 58 58
Freepost RSRB-KKBY-CYJK, PO Box 9090, STIRLING, FK8 2SA
Email: jo@samaritans.org

Mind
15-19 Broadway, Stratford, London E15 4BQ
Tel No: 020 8519 2122, Fax: 020 8522 1725
https://www.mind.org.uk/information-support/

Cancer Research
Tel No: 0300 123 1861
Email: supporter.services@cancer.org.uk

National Health Service – NHS Choices
https://www.nhs.uk/pages/home.aspx

Bibliography

1. **GOODREADS.COM**. (2018). *A quote from Sea of Swords*. [online] Available at: https://www.goodreads.com/quotes/122244-hinds ight-i-think-is-a-useless-tool-we-each-of [Accessed **22 Apr. 2018**].

2. **OFFICE FOR NATIONAL STATISTICS** *(ONS)*. Neighbourhood Statistics, *Retrieved 2012-12-22.*)

3. **20 WAYNE DYER QUOTES ABOUT LIFE.** Habits forwellbeing.com. (2017). *20 Wayne Dyer Quotes About Life*. [online] Available at: https://www.habitsforwellbeing. com/20-wayne-dyer-quotes-about-life/ [Accessed 30 Oct. 2017].

4. **ABRAHAM-HICKS QUOTES - LAW OF ATTRACTION RESOURCE GUIDE;** Law of Attraction Resource Guide. (2017). *Abraham-Hicks Quotes - Law of Attraction Resource Guide.* [online] Available at: https://www.lawofattraction-resourceguide.com/abraham-hicks-quotes/ [Accessed 30 Oct. 2017].

5. **BIBLE GATEWAY PASSAGE: MARK 12:41-44 - NEW INTERNATIONAL VERSION.** Bible Gateway. (2017). *Bible Gateway passage: Mark 12:41-44 - New International Version.* [online] Available at: https://www.biblegateway.com/passage/?search=Mark+12:41-44 [Accessed 30 Oct. 2017].

6. **PEMA CHÖDRÖN.** Goodreads.com. (2018). *When Things Fall Apart Quotes by Pema Chödrön.* [online] Available at: https://www.goodreads.com/work/quotes/2464740-when-things-fall-apart-heart-advice-for-difficult-times [Accessed 29 Jan. 2018].

7. **DEEPAK CHOPRA (@DEEPAKCHOPRA) | TWITTER.** Twitter.com. (2017). *Deepak Chopra (@DeepakChopra) | Twitter.* [online] Available at: https://twitter.com/DeepakChopra [Accessed 30 Oct. 2017].

8. **LOUISE HAY.** Louise Hay. (2018). The Power of Affirmations. [online] Available at: https://www.louisehay.com/the-power-of-affirmations/ [Accessed 27 Mar. 2018].

9. **ECKHART TOLLE TEACHINGS | HOW TO FREE YOURSELF FROM THE EGO.** Tolleteachings.com. (2017). *Eckhart Tolle Teachings | How to Free Yourself from the Ego.* [online] Available at: http://www.tolleteachings.com/freedom-from-ego.html [Accessed 30 Oct. 2017].

10. **MANDALA.** En.wikipedia.org. (2017). *Mandala.* [online] Available at: https://en.wikipedia.org/wiki/Mandala [Accessed 30 Oct. 2017].

11. **MICHAEL PRITCHARD FAMOUS QUOTE ABOUT GROW, LAUGHING, MATURITY, OLD, STOP | QUOTES DADDY** QuotesDaddy.com. (2017). Michael Pritchard Famous Quote about Grow, Laughing, Maturity, Old, Stop | Quotes Daddy. [online] Available at: https://www.quotesDaddy.com/quote/1133476/michael-pritchard/we-dont-stop-laughing-because-we-grow-old-we-grow [Accessed 30 Oct. 2017].

12. **NELSON MANDELA – WIKIQUOTE.** En.wikiquote.org. (2017). *Nelson Mandela - Wikiquote.* [online] Available at: https://en.wikiquote.org/wiki/Nelson_Mandela [Accessed 30 Oct. 2017].

13. **OSCAR M. LOPEZ, J.** The Course in Mastery Day 17: Self Esteem. Oscar M. Lopez, J. (2017). *The Course in Mastery Day 17: Self Esteem*. [online]. Ojmasterytv.blogspot.co.uk. Available at: http://ojmasterytv.blogspot.co.uk/2011/10/course-in-mastery-day-17-self-esteem.html [Accessed 30 Oct. 2017].

14. **PLOTNER, B.** Reprogramming The Brain For Desired Food Behavior - Nourishing Plot

15. Plotner, B. (2017). *Reprogramming The Brain for Desired Food Behavior - Nourishing Plot*. [online] Nourishing Plot. Available at: http://www.nourishingplot.com/2015/01/31/reprogramming-the-brain-for-desired-food-behavior/ [Accessed 30 Oct. 2017].

16. **SHAYGAN, L.** 7 Ways to Benefit from Not Getting What You Want Shaygan, L. (2017). *7 Ways to Benefit from Not Getting What You Want*. [online] Tiny Buddha. Available at: https://tinybuddha.com/blog/7-ways-to-benefit-from-not-getting-what-you-want/ [Accessed 30 Oct. 2017].

17. **UP FROM SLAVERY: AN AUTOBIOGRAPHY BY BOOKER T. WASHINGTON: CHAPTER 2 (CONTINUED) - THE LITERATURE PAGE.** Literaturepage.com. (2017). *Up from Slavery: An Autobiography by Booker T. Washington: Chapter 2 (continued) - The Literature Page*. [online] Available at: http://www.literaturepage.com/read/upfromslavery-32.html [Accessed 30 Oct. 2017].

18. **DENIS WAITLEY QUOTES.** Abundance-and-happiness.com. (2017). *Denis Waitley Quotes*. [online] Available at: http://www.abundance-and-happiness.com/denis-waitley-quotes.html [Accessed 30 Oct. 2017].

19. **WALT DISNEY QUOTES.** BrainyQuote. (2017). *Walt Disney. Quotes*. [online] Available at: https://www.brainyquote.com/quotes/quotes/w/waltdisney163027.html [Accessed 30 Oct. 2017].

20. **ALEXANDER POPE.** An Essay on Criticism. En.wikipedia.org. (2018). Fools rush in where angels fear to tread. [online] Available at: https://en.wikipedia.org/wiki/Fools_Rush_In_Where_Angels_Fear_to_Tread [Accessed 27 Mar. 2018].

Index

riches, 11
rising, 23
rocky, 1, 28
rollercoaster, 31
Romford, 34
root chakra, 138, 140, 146, 148
running, xvi, 17, 42, 53-55, 60, 91, 100, 112

S
sacked, 38
sacral chakra, 138, 141, 148
sacrifice, 4
sad, 8, 11, 14-15, 19, 50, 72, 88, 93, 107, 123
safe, 9, 12, 29, 59, 103, 140
salon, 54-56
Sandwich, 32
Sanskrit, 136, 138
satisfaction, 62
scared, 55
scenarios, 18, 53, 108, 116
scent, 8, 10-11, 42
school, xv, xvi, 30-32, 36, 39-40, 47, 57, 59-60, 68, 82, 108
screaming, xvi, 77
scrub, 100, 120
Sea Cadets, 30
seafront, 35
search, 59, 152
secure, 16, 29, 112
seeking, 3, 122
self, 2, 19, 58, 133, 138, 146-147, 152
self-expression, 144
self-healing, 16
selfish, 3, 61, 84
selfless, 84, 118, 119
self-preservation, 140, 148
self-scrutiny, 144
sell, 13, 35, 45, 96
senior, 28, 48

sensation, 79, 91, 109, 135, 150
sense, 1-2, 9-10, 13-14, 20, 22-23, 25, 33, 40, 60, 84, 94, 101, 116, 133, 145, 147-149, 151-152
sensuality, 141
serve, 4, 21, 59, 116-117, 119, 121, 142
share, xvii, xix, 2, 15, 18, 84, 95, 99, 106, 155
Shaygan, 81
shift, 13, 61, 102, 127, 133-134, 152
shingles, 49, 93
shock, 51, 66, 69, 71, 73
sifting, 13
sight, 1, 3-4, 9, 24
sign, 33, 43, 72-73, 79, 92, 109, 135
silence, 30
sing, 8, 16, 28, 117, 140
sisters, 65
sitting, 10, 25, 43-44, 46, 73, 112, 140
situation, 15, 17-19, 24-25, 29, 36, 42, 47, 51, 62, 64, 72, 77, 81, 84-86, 103, 120, 127-128, 131
skin, xvi, 10, 67, 100, 110, 118-121
sleep, 18, 24, 73, 90, 94, 99, 101, 140
slimming, 30
smell, 1, 8, 10, 106, 109-110, 136, 151
soap opera, 116
social life, 31-32
social networking, 144
society, 82, 84, 102, 107, 109, 118
soft, 33, 134-135

About the Author

Donella started her Health and Wellness business at twenty one after achieving 'student of the year award' at college for the courses she had completed. A few years later, having established her salon, unforeseen changes forced her to leave and she took this opportunity to pursue a teaching career in beauty and holistic therapy before completing her education to obtain her teaching degree.

She served her local community with health and beauty services working with a range of clients living in sheltered accommodation, those who required a mobile service and those who visited her home salon where she worked around her family, as a mother of two. She often volunteered for local Charites to support charity fund raising events including the Air Ambulance, the National Childbirth Trust, Cancer Research and others.

Any parent who has run a business whilst looking after children will know that this is a balancing act. Donella thrived on this—she was teaching, running her health and wellbeing business and undertaking further training on Yoga, then Pilates, which she took to the next level by qualifying as a teacher.

She continues her health and wellbeing business under the name *Transform your life with Donella*. She offers mind and body treatments and beauty training courses. She also teaches Yoga, Pilates, Stretch and Relax and Meditation to likeminded souls using her expertise, enthusiasm and dedication to help others to restore balance and keep their bodies in optimum condition.

She incorporates meditations that she writes into practices for reflection to help clients refocus and re-centre their lives. Although Donella has experienced turbulence in her life—suffering racism, eating disorders, physical and mental abuse and several toxic relationships, she gained strength in adversity. Knowing that there is always a solution to a problem, there is always hope, there is always a way to change, to restore self-love and self-worth.

Visit her website at www.transformyourlifewithdonella.com where you can find out more about the full range of services and meditation downloads available.